Legislatures and the
New Democracies
in Latin America

Legislatures and the New Democracies in Latin America

edited by
David Close

LYNNE
RIENNER
PUBLISHERS

BOULDER
LONDON

Published in the United States of America in 1995 by
Lynne Rienner Publishers, Inc.
1800 30th Street, Boulder, Colorado 80301

and in the United Kingdom by
Lynne Rienner Publishers, Inc.
3 Henrietta Street, Covent Garden, London WC2E 8LU

Library of Congress Cataloging-in-Publication Data
Legislatures and the new democracies in Latin America / edited by
    David Close.
        p. cm.
    Includes bibliographical references and index.
    ISBN 1-55587-475-4 (alk. paper)
    1. Legislative bodies—Latin America. 2. Democracy—Latin
America. 3. Latin America—Politics and government—1980–
I. Close, David, 1945–
JL963.L44 1995
328.8'07—dc20   94-42491
                                             CIP

British Cataloguing in Publication Data
A Cataloguing in Publication record for this book
is available from the British Library.

Printed and bound in the United States of America

⊗ The paper used in this publication meets the requirements
    of the American National Standard for Permanence of
    Paper for Printed Library Materials Z39.48–1984.

5 4 3 2 1

Contents

Foreword

The Honourable John Bosley, P.C., M.P.

In the spring of 1988, I had the honor to chair a special committee of the House of Commons on the peace process in Central America. The resulting report, supported by all parties in the House, stressed the importance of human rights and democratic development to the achievement of lasting peace in Central America. The committee recommended that Canada provide special support for the development of a Central American parliament.

As a former speaker of the House of Commons and a member of Parliament for fourteen years, I have no illusions about the grandeur or perfectibility of legislatures. They can be parochial and narrowly partisan institutions that reinforce divisions within and between countries. Nonetheless, they are a vital part of the infrastructure of democracy, arguably *the* vital part, because they gather together representatives of the various interests and ideological tendencies in a society and test their collective ability to reconcile differences. The emergence of a democratic culture depends in no small part on whether and how that reconciliation is accomplished.

Given the importance of legislatures, and their comparative neglect in the literature of development, I am delighted that David Close has organized this collection of essays on the role of legislatures in democratic transitions in Latin America.

Acronyms

AD   Democratic Action

CD   Democratic Convergence

MAC   Christian Action Movement

MNR   National Revolutionary Movement

MPSC   Popular Social Christian Movement

PARM   Authentic Party of the Mexican Revolution

PCD   Christian Democratic Party

PCN   Party of National Conciliation

PDM   Mexican Democratic Party

PFCRN   Party of the Cardenista Front for National Reconstruction

PMT   Mexican Workers' Party

PPS   Popular Socialist Party

PRT   Revolutionary Workers' Party

PSD   Social Democratic Party

PST   Socialist Workers' Party

Introduction: Consolidating Democracy in Latin America— What Role for Legislatures?

David Close

Not very long ago a book about Latin American legislatures would have been dismissed as a pointless venture into the trivial. Latin American politics have now changed enough that attention to the assembly is both useful and necessary. This book starts from that premise, but goes further, to include the notion that legislatures in the democratizing states of Latin America offer a valuable perspective on the changing political system as a whole. In particular, it takes the position that analyzing legislatures can be an especially useful way to approach questions of democratic transition and consolidation.

Viewing democratization through the legislative window draws the observer's attention to several key areas. First, examining parliament shows if there are interests or opinions that are grossly over- or under-represented, thus providing a rough estimate of the polity's inclusiveness. Second, looking at legislatures gives a sense of how and how well those in power are held accountable for their acts, an inchoate measure of a system's constitutionalism. Third, the proceedings of representative assemblies help us gauge the conflict that arises over public issues and show how effectively that conflict is resolved, thus offering an initial indicator of a country's ability to manage political contention and dissent.

There is a further, more practical reason to fix on legislatures: they and the rest of the institutional apparatus of liberal democracy are becoming prominent parts of increasing numbers of political systems. Each of the many countries currently embarked on a democratizing project has opted for liberal, representative democracy; not the radical, participatory democracy pursued in the past. This makes students of Third World and Eastern European politics regard the orthodox machinery of democratic government afresh, and ask how it will function in its new settings.

In this regard, the current era recalls the 1950s and 1960s, when there was a scholarly interest in political development that included studies of how the conventional institutions of developed democratic states performed in poor countries without democratic histories. That venture paid few dividends, largely because liberal democracy so often failed; but the project should be taken up again—stripped, to be sure, of the unconscious ethnocentric baggage it then carried. There is little more exciting for a political scientist than watching attempts at constructing constitutional, liberal states and the machinery that makes them work: the coevolution of ideas, culture, process, and institutions. The seven case studies presented here (Argentina, Brazil, Chile, El Salvador, Mexico, Nicaragua, and Uruguay) offer a start on that enterprise in Latin America.

Legislatures as "Efficient Parts" of Liberal Democracies

In his 1867 study of English politics, Walter Bagehot distinguishes between the "dignified" and "efficient" parts of a political system.[1] Dignified elements conferred legitimacy, but had little part in the daily operations of government. In contrast, the efficient parts were what actually ran the country.

Latin American legislatures have, with rare exceptions,[2] been found on the dignified side of the ledger. Usually subordinate to the executive, sometimes to the point of functional irrelevance, legislatures did pass laws and provide posts for the party faithful,[3] but they were peripheral to the business of governing. Now, however, most Latin American states have opted for liberal democratic forms that demand effective legislatures. In developed democracies, legislatures carry out five functions that make them efficient in Bagehot's sense: lawmaking; overseeing the executive; publicizing issues; representing varied currents of opinion; and managing and resolving conflicts.

The first thing a legislature must do to be an efficient part of government (what Martin Needler calls a "serious legislature" in his conclusion to this collection) is make laws. At a minimum this requires that most of a country's laws come not from executive decrees but from bills duly debated and approved by a representative body. This does *not* mean that the legislature must actually compose and propose a program of laws, as does the U.S. Congress. The constitutions of the parliamentary systems common to Britain, the British Commonwealth, and Western Europe do not permit this.[4] A useful rule of thumb is that where legislative bills, not executive orders, are the preponderant source of public law, the legislature is a lawmaker.

A second function an "efficient" legislature performs is ensuring the accountability of the executive. Though elections are a liberal democracy's ultimate weapon for keeping its rulers answerable to citizens, they happen infrequently. In the period between elections other institutions take this role. Although the media report on all areas of public affairs, the legislature assumes particular responsibility for keeping tabs on the executive parts of government. John Stuart Mill gives great prominence to this function in *Representative Government:*

> The proper office of a representative assembly is to watch and control the government; to throw the light of publicity on its acts; to compel a full exposition and justification of all of them which any one considers questionable; to censure them if found condemnable.[5]

Legislatures do this in several ways. Perhaps the most recognizable way is through the budget power. An assembly that can defeat or amend a national budget is, other things being equal, a more potent force than one that only debates the document.[6] Even in the latter case, however, skilful legislators can expose biases and inconsistencies in an executive's financial plans that voters recall at the next election.

Scrutiny of the executive also takes place through either a question period or the summoning of cabinet members before legislative committees. Not all legislatures have both tools at their disposal, but any legislature that is an efficient part of government possesses one of them. These powers let the legislature inform both itself and the public about the operations of government.

This publicizing function of legislatures is frequently overshadowed by today's investigative journalism and sophisticated electronic media. Yet a substantial part of the evening news in liberal democracies is generated by the day's parliamentary debates or hearings. Moreover, following a bill through the legislature lets a citizen glimpse a part of the country's policymaking process. In fact, legislative proceedings are probably the most public part of a liberal democracy's policy process; certainly they generate the most intense public criticism and debate. And public figures must take public stands on public issues before citizens can judge their actions.

Besides informing citizens, a legislature that is an efficient part of a democratic political system must also represent them. Though this is not the place to analyze the concept of representation,[7] it is patent that a state cannot systematically exclude important segments of its citizens from participation in policymaking and remain a democracy. Indeed, such a state is unlikely even to remain administratively effective because a government that cannot tap the sentiments of significant parts of the population will make bad policies that are hard to enforce. Performing this representative function satisfactorily demands that certain prerequisites be met. The most important of these are equitable districting and an electoral system that does not consciously deny access to identifiable groups.[8]

Obviously, a substantial part of the legislature's representativeness is beyond the institution's control. No parliament can order a political party to seek the votes or express the concerns of an interest that the party chooses to ignore. But an assembly that has some political weight can spur neglected sectors to either form their own party or become sufficiently evident that an existing party will want them as adherents.[9]

The final function that a contemporary efficient legislature performs is conflict management. John Wahlke suggests that a key role of any legislature is to identify a society's political conflicts and reduce them to manageable levels.[10] As with so much else legislatures do, this role is performed differently in different systems. All legislatures use highly stylized forms of address and complex rules of debate to limit tension. Where party discipline is weak, as in the United States or mid-nineteenth century Britain, an extra instrument is available, as individual legislators may broker deals on bills. Even in systems where party discipline is tightly enforced, committee systems are sometimes structured to let compromises arise that cabinets later incorporate into government bills.[11]

Legislatures are plainly important instruments of actually existing democracies. They inform citizens about government actions, allow politicians to find broadly acceptable solutions to public problems, limit the executive's arrogation of power, and bring together a wide enough spectrum of a nation's politically salient interests to make a plausible claim to represent the opinions of a nation's citizens. Citizens of stable liberal democracies accept the presence of an active legislature as a given, but they seldom reflect on the centrality of the legislature in the struggle for democracy in Europe and North America. It is to this "democracy-building" side of legislatures that we now turn.

Legislatures and Democratization: A Historical Perspective

The roles legislatures take in functioning democracies have developed over the centuries. Representative assemblies are predemocratic in origin, but within the Anglo-American political tradition they have long been associated with resistance to absolutism and tyranny. Though this view may be overly romantic, it does have a basis in fact.

From the moment England's Edward I convened knights, citizens, and burgesses to his first general parliament in 1275, the scope of the royal prerogative began to shrink and the realm of publicly made law to expand.[12] This marked the origins of citizens' control over their rulers in the Western world.

Heroic pages in the history of liberty were written by revolutionary assemblies in the United States and France in the late eighteenth century. Less dramatic, but no less important to the construction of democracy in North America and Western Europe, were the many battles fought in nineteenth-century legislatures to expand the franchise, recognize the right of labor to organize, and place the first limits on the privileges of birth and wealth. Though these struggles were not complete until the middle of this century, legislatures provided sites *within the constitutional order* where issues of great democratic moment could be joined. Two of the five general functions of a politically significant legislature merit special attention in relation to democratization.

It is best to begin with oldest democratic role of a legislature: restricting the arbitrary exercise of royal authority. The pertinence of this role in countries swept up in Huntington's "third wave of democracy"[13] is apparent. The old, authoritarian regimes in these countries were all strongly executive-centered. Establishing democracy there demands that the executive's power be countervailed and controlled by constitutional means. This is the same lesson the framers of the U.S. Constitution drew from their observations of eighteenth-century British political history, and it can be taken equally well today by architects of democracy from Russia to Guatemala.

However, controlling the political executive is only part of how legislatures helped establish democracy. A second important element was their representation of an increasingly universal citizenry. The democratic potential of representative government was sufficiently obvious to eighteenth- and nineteenth-century constitution makers that they added second chambers that were indirectly elected (the U.S. Senate until 1913) or appointed (the Canadian Senate) to ensure that the demands of the majority would be buffered by more conservative elements.[14]

Again, the applicability of this history to the present is plain. Where politics has been the preserve of magnates, dictators, military men, or revolutionary vanguards, ordinary people have been left on the sidelines. Making a democratic future plausible requires finding ways to let average citizens make their demands known. Legislatures added this task to their duties as liberal democracies evolved in the nineteenth century.

Over time, legislatures became integral, institutionalized parts of their national political systems. At some point, it became impossible for a president or prime minister to suspend the assembly's sittings, send the legislators home, and rule by decree. To get to this point, however, legislatures had to learn to maintain a delicate balance between elite and democratic interests. They could not too radically challenge the economic, political, and social establishment, for to do so would risk sowing the seeds of reaction. Neither, however, could assemblies fail to represent the masses and deliver some tangible benefits to them.

What let legislatures find this balance, and so permit the creation of representative democracies in Western Europe and North America, was a fortunate combination of economic expansion and able leadership. Economic growth gave elites a measure of material security that made concessions to the middle classes and the poor easier to accept. Able leaders recognized that it would be easier to accommodate the majority than prepare the elite for an endless political siege. If this reading of history is accurate it suggests that the world's new democracies need luck and leadership as well as the right institutions to prosper.

In fact, another caveat is in order: legislatures, even when strong and institutionalized—that is, efficient parts of the system—do not guarantee democracy. They can pass abusive laws, defend the establishment, and willfully ignore the needs of the weak and marginalized. One need only think of the horrors that members of the British Parliament or U.S. Congress, elected by broadly democratic constituencies, have worked to appreciate this. Moreover, a legislature can produce political stasis, either because its members cannot form themselves into a stable majority or because it, as a body, has entered into an irreconcilable conflict with the executive. Under the wrong circumstances, the resulting deadlock can delegitimate democracy itself. And there is always a danger that electors will return to the legislature parties whose commitment to democracy is questionable. The recent emergence of far right political parties in Europe is one example, and the chapter on Nicaragua in this collection presents another.

Legislatures and Democratic Consolidation in Latin America

How does a legislature contribute to building liberal democracies in contemporary Latin America? The dramatic days of establishing new constitutional democracies, when the focus was understandably on elections, are now past, save in Cuba, Haiti, and perhaps Mexico. Most countries in Latin America now face the lengthier task of making open polities work: democratic transitions have become exercises in democratic consolidation. The foregoing section lays out some of the things that representative assemblies have done to build democracies in the liberal democratic heartlands. Yet there may be factors specific to Latin America, or even to this third wave of democratization, that could keep the legislature from repeating its earlier role, thereby jeopardizing the prospects for developing representative democracies.

The first and most controversial of these is the region's long history of centralized authority.[15] That Latin America shares this trait with most of the Third World, Central and Eastern Europe and Russia, and preindustrial Western Europe only makes it more pressing to consider its effects. The chapters in this book on Mexico and Argentina suggest that centralism, in the form of extreme executive-centeredness, has become a core part of those nations' political cultures (though this book's conclusion warns against reading this to mean that democracy is thereby precluded). This debate over the content and influence of political culture on Latin American politics is irresolvable, but a couple of points about the potential relationship between political culture and the role of legislatures merit attention.

One is simply that strongly executive-centered, authoritarian states have developed strong legislatures and robust liberal democracies. Spain and Portugal are only the latest additions to a list that goes back to Britain. The question thus has to be what makes things change.

A start at an answer comes in the chapters on El Salvador and Nicaragua. In the latter country, the legislature has become an independent political force able to make the president's life difficult, whereas the former country's chamber seems content to continue its passive, even submissive, role. Although the personalities of the presidents, the characteristics of the political parties, and the specific issues confronted in each country obviously have an influence, there is another variable at work.

If, historically, the executive is where power lies and decisions are made, that is where citizens will look for leadership and ambitious politicians will fix their attention. However, should that power be unattainable, as it was to the knights, citizens, and burgesses Edward I convened seven centuries ago, practical politicians turn elsewhere to work their designs. Often the legislature is the tool that falls most readily to hand. This is essentially what happened in Nicaragua. Legislators dissatisfied with the president's program, but unable to get her to amend it and unwilling or unable to resort to a military coup, have tried to turn the country's National Assembly into an agency capable of enacting and implementing their agenda. Though this has not yet made

Nicaragua a constitutional democracy, it has for the first time given the country a legislature that counts for something in national politics.

Less controversial theoretically but no less pressing practically is the matter of how a democratizing legislature will respond to conjunctural problems. Two of these, controlling the military and effecting national reconciliation, are especially important.

The legislature should be a splendid device for ensuring civilian control over the military because it votes on the budget. Yet the military may seek to declare itself a "reserved domain," exempt from legislative control, or even claim "tutelary powers" in the form of a veto over government actions, thus provoking a confrontation with the legislature. Though not as dangerous to the democratic regime as a military veto, bitter wrangling that deadlocks the legislature can arise over what to do with often lavish military appropriations.[16]

Legislatures also ought to be admirably placed to reconcile the bitter differences that are the legacies of bureaucratic authoritarian rule in South America and protracted civil conflict in Central America. For that to happen, however, the legislators themselves must be prepared to use the assembly as an arena for conflict resolution and not marshal majorities to punish old enemies. What legislatures do to advance or retard democratization depends not just on their institutional capacities, but on the conduct of the deputies who sit in them, and even on the nature of the political and social systems in which the legislatures and their members work.

The Framework

Seven countries serve as case studies: Argentina, Brazil, Chile, El Salvador, Mexico, Nicaragua, and Uruguay. All are conventionally described as being democratizing regimes, but they possess strikingly diverse histories and contrasting social, economic, and political characteristics. These differences ensure a thorough survey of the conditions under which legislatures work in Latin America's transitional polities.

Because the studies center on the legislature, they all adopt an institutional approach that is substantially state-centered. But showing the legislature in its full political context demands going beyond institutional description to identify and trace the development of the array of forces that affect political life.[17] Consequently, these are *not* conventional "legislative studies" that examine the assembly's functioning as an end in itself. Rather, each presents a national legislature fitting into an *evolving* political system. The aim is to depict the legislature's relations with the rest of the polity (the executive, extraparliamentary forces, the media, and national political traditions and customs) as well as its internal operations (party representation, organization and rules, and majority-minority relations). The legislature becomes both a subject *of* inquiry (in terms of its own structure and operations) and an input *to* inquiry (regarding its role in the broader political system and its impact on democratic construction).

Directing attention away from the nuts and bolts of legislative organization and behavior is salutary, even essential, here. The representative bodies in these states are still searching for their identities as democratic institutions. They are, in most instances, inchoate versions of democratic legislatures, just as the political systems of which they are parts are not yet fully fledged democracies. To focus too closely on their specific dynamics would risk both losing sight of the milieux in which they function and giving a description that would soon be inaccurate. We want to know what legislatures contribute, positively or negatively, to the building of democracy in seven countries, a project requiring approaches different from those used to study legislatures in established constitutional democracies.

One other methodological note: combining the paucity of studies of Latin American legislatures (either single-country or comparative analyses) with the newness of studies of democratic consolidation meant that the authors had to create empirical baselines for their studies. Accordingly, there is a strong descriptive component in each of the country analyses. Further, factors emphasized in one chapter may be glossed over in the next, simply because of national differences. Though this produces an empirical richness that will please many Latin Americanists, it may frustrate political scientists whose interest is legislative behavior. This trade-off, though, is one of the many costs of trying to analyze democratization in process.

The Cases

Each case study describes the status of the national legislature as it stood in late 1993, and the order of the studies' presentation follows geography, running from north to south. Mexico has taken the fewest steps away from its old regime; both of the Central American states have histories innocent of representative democracy and redolent of recent insurgent conflict; the four Southern Cone countries share the experience of military, bureaucratic authoritarianism. Geography thus reflects political features that bear on the countries' democratic prospects.

In Mexico a break with the past is less clear than in the other six nations. Its polity is executive-dominated and substantially controlled by the historic party of government, the Institutional Revolutionary Party (PRI). This system has left little room for legislative oversight of the executive or for Mexico's congress to emerge as the nation's center of political debate, much less assume any independent lawmaking capacity. And because the legislature is not a key player in Mexican politics, ambitious politicians have not chosen it as their road to power.

Yet Roderic Camp's analysis of legislative politics in Mexico (Chapter 1) indicates that the very marginalization of the congress made the body the principal focus for liberalizing reforms undertaken since the 1970s. Unwilling to loosen its hold on the executive, the PRI leadership concentrated its efforts to open the system squarely on the congress. Though the government has acted since the notorious election of 1988 to counteract the effects of those liberalizing changes, there was still hope that the accumulated reforms of two decades would prove a durable base for future democratic experiments. Whether this remains true after the dramatic and tragic events of early 1994—the rebellion in Chiapas and the assassination of PRI presidential candidate Luis Donaldo Colosio—is one of the many unknowns plaguing contemporary Mexican politics. Still, studying Mexico provides clues about how a representative assembly might contribute to the slow opening of an uncompetitive polity.

In El Salvador and Nicaragua the links to the past have been broken and the old regimes dismissed. There the legislatures are parts of new constitutional orders engaged in constructing what may or may not prove to be the foundations of representative, liberal democracy. These two Central American states share several traits that cloud their democratic prospects. Neither has much historical experience with representative government; both fought counterinsurgencies throughout the 1980s, so both now face major tasks of reconciliation and reconstruction; and though El Salvador is economically stronger than Nicaragua, both confront the future with meager material resources. But there is one great difference that separates them: El Salvador started its journey toward constitutional democracy from the oligarchic right and Nicaragua from the revolutionary left. The obvious question is whether either of those regimes provided a sound foundation for representative democracy.

José Garcia's examination of El Salvador in Chapter 2 reveals a legislature that has always been subordinate to the real power holders in that country: armed forces, oligarchies, dictators, and now political parties. Historically weak and more deferential toward real power than respectful of legal authority, this assembly can do no more than *reflect* the political power of critical actors. Garcia sees little chance that this will change. He argues that although the Salvadoran legislature may become more technically competent, it will not become a political force in its own right.

Nicaragua's recent experience has been very different, as discussed in Chapter 3. The National Assembly has been not just autonomous, but positively assertive. During the first three years of the Chamorro presidency, the legislature was locked in seemingly perpetual conflict with the executive. These confrontations produced as by-products a leader who used the legislature first to build a national reputation and later as the springboard for an attempted coup against the constitutional order. Active and autonomous legislatures do not, then, always contribute to building a functioning democracy. Thus, a judgment issued at this point would be hard pressed to specify whether Nicaragua's legislature had, on balance, contributed more or less to democratic consolidation over the past several years than had El Salvador's.

The remaining case studies focus on the former bureaucratic authoritarian states of South America: Argentina, Brazil, Chile, and Uruguay. All countries bore the burden of transformational military authoritarian rule; but Chile and Uruguay have long histories as constitutional democracies, whereas Argentina and Brazil do not. Here the obvious question is whether the legislature's current role in each country reflects these historical differences.

Argentina, like Mexico and El Salvador, hosts a regime that Gary Wynia in Chapter 4 calls "hyperpresidentialist." As a predictable correlate, if not consequence, the country's congress is institutionally weak and viewed by the president as a chamber to ratify his policies. The persistence of a personalist presidentialism in which the chief executive ignores the usual institutional checks and balances prompts Wynia to ask if Argentine citizens want an autonomous legislature or are happier with a strong, unencumbered president. This suggests that a political culture that accommodates a highly individualistic and powerful presidency may not easily understand or accept attempts to put limits on the executive.[18]

Though Brazil's congress functions in the same executive-centered environment as its Argentine neighbor, it has a much more eventful recent past. Though it is easy enough to think of the Brazilian legislature impeaching former president Fernando Collor de Mello, Daniel Zirker reminds us in Chapter 5 that the congress was also an important player during the military regime. Unlike the other Southern Cone military authoritarians, Brazil's soldier politicians permitted licensed political parties to function within a legislature designed to be similarly licensed. Yet from 1965 to 1985 the Congress did more than legitimate the dictatorship; it functioned as a safety valve for political pressures and, along the way, acquired an unearned reputation as a democratic vehicle.

Perhaps it was this democratic aura that resulted in the 1988 constitution strengthening Congress. At first, this seemed to pay off, because Congress did pursue its impeachment of President Collor. But within a year, in late 1993, the assembly was rocked by a massive corruption scandal, destroying the legitimacy it had earlier acquired. Zirker concludes that the legislature has not lost its historic commitment to blocking substantive reforms and that it remains "risk-averse" and "elite-oriented." Brazil's Congress was a weak institution in the past and remains so today, unable or unwilling to lead even when the country is without a strong president.

Chile and Uruguay are distinguished from the other countries in this survey because they have actually enjoyed periods of representative government and are thus seeking to "reconsolidate" constitutional democratic rule. Common sense suggests that, when each shed its military dictatorship, old habits would reassert themselves and again produce effective legislatures. However, this ignores the possible effects of a long span of rigid authoritarianism on a country's institutions.

Jorge Nef and Nibaldo Galleguillos argue persuasively in Chapter 6 that the rupture with democracy in 1973 in Chile outweighs the country's history of constitutionalism. The Pinochet regime bequeathed the country an institutional framework that left the armed forces in a privileged political position and guaranteed that Chileans would enjoy only restricted democracy. Part of that guarantee takes the form of nine senators appointed by the military dictatorship to serve until 1997, enough to join elected conservatives and make democratizing the constitution impossible.

The dictatorship's constitutional handiwork was enough to keep reform at bay during the first post–democratic restoration Aylwin administration. However, the 1993 elections returned a large enough contingent of democrats to ally with the new Frei government and discard the legacy of Pinochet. Nef and Galleguillos caution, though, that even congressional deputies elected on democratic platforms may find it too hard to break "the pact of elites" that sustains Chile's "low-intensity democracy" and so may opt to defend the status quo ante.

In Chapter 7 Martin Weinstein argues that Uruguay's legislature is important because constitutional democracy is taken seriously. This may seem a truism, but it is what sustains the authority of the legislature in Britain, Canada, and the United States. Uruguay's representative assembly is part of a clearly president-dominant polity, hardly novel in Latin America. What is exceptional is that this legislature is better known as an effective instrument for the defense of the rule of law and civil liberties than of entrenched privilege.

Weinstein locates the roots of representative government in Uruguay's electoral system, which encourages the fractionalization seen in the party system. This produces not just a multifactional legislature, but also returns presidents whose mandates rest on smallish pluralities instead of overwhelming majorities. Consensus must be sought for the system to work; the fact that consensus is often found, Weinstein suggests, reflects Uruguayan political culture. The result is that in Uruguay the legislature has resumed a political role familiar to citizens of established liberal democracies: it raises issues, locks horns with the executive, and is a normal, active part of the political process.

In his concluding essay, Martin Needler lays out guidelines for reflection on the themes raised in this collection. Key among these is his reminder that we are now witnessing the most democratic era in Latin American history. Never before have there been fewer dictatorships, restless armies, or nervous U.S. foreign policy makers retarding free government.

At its best, this means that more countries may start taking constitutional democracy seriously. Needler notes that presidents Fernando Collor of Brazil and Carlos Andrés Pérez of Venezuela were dismissed from office by impeachment and not coups, and he suggests that these actions "may represent a genuinely new stage in the political evolution of the region." Though this new stage promises a greater role for Latin America's legislatures, Needler admonishes us not to lose sight of the fact that "the legislature is embedded in a particular structure of power and its role has to be understood in relation to that system of power." The end product, a democratic political system, counts for far more than any institutional adjustments done to raise the assembly's profile.

The lesson that emerges from these studies is that legislatures now merit attention. They are seldom the key players in democratizing Latin American polities, but neither are they insignificant ciphers. Further, the findings reported here remind us that simply because an assembly is politically important does not mean that it is advancing the cause of democracy. A stronger representative branch can use its powers to retard democracy by pushing elite agendas and thwarting popular initiatives; the executive parts of government have no monopoly on knavery.

If, however, constitutional democracy is to succeed there must be legislatures that bring together a nation's significant political interests while ensuring that historically unaccountable executives begin to answer for their decisions. These are challenging tasks that can be carried out only by institutions with substantial legal, material, and human resources. Legislatures thus must be powerful, and wherever power exists so does the chance that it can be turned to wicked ends. Unfortunately, there is no formula to ensure that a stronger legislature in any of the countries studied here will try to emulate the British Parliament or U.S. Congress, which despite their many flaws do at least provide the minimal requirements of constitutional government. What is certain, though, is that weak legislatures will neither bring accountability to government nor guarantee fair representation.

Notes

1. Walter Bagehot, *The English Constitution* (London: Fontana, 1967 [1867]). Bagehot sees both dignified (the monarchy) and efficient (the cabinet) parts of government as necessary for the state to work well. Thus it is a mistake to assume that the dignified elements, "those which excite and preserve the reverence of the population" (Bagehot, p. 63), do not matter or are not "institutionalized" parts of the political system. Thus, when speaking of the legislature as belonging to the "efficient" side of a political system, we mean that it ordinarily affects how policy is made.

2. Among the exceptions would be Chile from 1890 to 1924 and contemporary Costa Rica.

3. See, José Garcia, Chapter 2 of this book; Knut Walter, *The Regime of Anastasio Somoza, 1936–1956* (Chapel Hill: University of North Carolina Press, 1993).

4. The actual differences in the legislative function between presidential and parliamentary systems may be overstated because delegated legislation—laws passed by the legislature in framework form to be filled in by the executive departments—is such an important part of any assembly's work.

5. John Stuart Mill, *Representative Government,* in *Utilitarianism. Liberty. Representative Government.* (London: J. M Dent & Sons, Ltd., 1910 [1861]), p. 239.

6. Of course, all other things are *not* equal. Though the Canadian Parliament normally just debates the government's budget, defeating even one section of the document signifies want of confidence, defeats the government, and sends the country to an election. This last happened in December 1979.

7. The best treatment of this issue is Hanna Pitkin, *The Concept of Representation* (Berkeley: University of California Press, 1972).

8. I leave aside the question of an electoral system designed to exclude antisystem groups, via either legal proscription or a discriminatory electoral system (e.g., a threshold of votes that must be attained before a party can receive a seat).

9. Evidence of this is presented in Chapter 3 of this book.

10. "Policy Determinants and Legislative Decisions," in S. Ulmer (ed.), *Political Decision-Making* (New York: Van Nostrand, 1970), p. 108.

11. A thorough examination of one example of this is found in D. Close, *Legislative Consultation: Standing Committees in the Quebec National Assembly,* unpublished Ph.D. diss., McGill University, Montreal, Quebec, 1978.

12. A useful brief reference is Kenneth Mackenzie, *The English Parliament* (Hammersmith: Penguin, 1962). A more thorough standard source is J.E.A. Jolliffe, *The Constitutional History of Medieval England* (New York: Norton, 1961).

13. Samuel Huntington, *The Third Wave* (Norman: University of Oklahoma Press, 1991).

14. Canada's first prime minister, Sir John A. Macdonald, once observed that the function of the country's Senate was to protect its permanent minority, the rich.

15. Important statements emphasizing the importance of political tradition are contained in Howard Wiarda (ed.), *Politics and Social Change in Latin America: The Distinct Tradition* (Amherst: University of Massachusetts Press, 1982).

16. The concepts of tutelary powers and reserved domains are from J. Samuel Valenzuela, "Democratic Consolidation in Post-Transitional Settings: Notion, Process, and Facilitating Conditions," in *Issues in Democratic Consolidation,* ed. by S. Mainwaring, G. O'Donnell, and J. S. Valenzuela (Notre Dame, Indiana: University of Notre Dame Press, 1992), pp. 57–104. For an instance of a legislature turning the military budget into a partisan football, see Chapter 3 of this volume.

17. The methods used here are compatible with the political interaction framework elaborated by Chazan, et al. This approach "focuses on identifying the multiple factors at work on . . . the political scene and tracing their diverse dynamics over time." N. Chazan, R. Mortimer, J. Ravenhill, and D. Rothchild, *Politics and Society in Contemporary Africa,* 2d edition (Boulder: Lynne Rienner, 1992), p. 23.

18. Russia is another country where citizens apparently prefer a strong, even autocratic, leader. However, Nicaragua's experience indicates how quickly a preference for a strong executive can turn into support for a powerful legislature when conditions warrant. A sudden embrace of the virtues of representative government may only be opportunism on the part of disgruntled elites, but it can still shift the historic balance between the executive and legislative branches in a country.

1

Mexico's Legislature: Missing the Democratic Lockstep?

Roderic Camp

The political world in Latin America and Europe has witnessed the globalization of democratic change, what some scholars have described as the Americanization of elections.[1] Although presidential contests are not the sole form of election, they receive most of the media attention. In contrast, generally speaking, legislatures tend to represent, at least symbolically speaking, democratic polities. Their institutional changes and breadth of representation measure even more deeply the commitment to democratization.

Much has been made of recent alterations in political practices in Central and South America, especially in Brazil, Chile, Argentina, El Salvador, and Nicaragua. In the latter two cases, the United States has even taken some credit for their political restructuring. I would argue, however, that many of these changes are more superficial than real, and that elections alone are an inadequate measure of democratization.[2] Many of these countries, especially Nicaragua and El Salvador, have imposed electoral processes and representative structures on political cultures that lack a firm basis of support for democratic principles. Nevertheless, it is fair to say that these and other Latin American countries are, if only temporarily, moving in a democratic direction.[3] The vitality of this movement appears most clearly in the legislative branch, where give and take, debate, and compromise are witnessed daily. Why then is Mexico—the country closest to the United States, the culture most influenced by the United States, and the society most vulnerable to U.S. economic and political decisions—even more resistant to both superficial and deep structural revisions? Why has the legislative branch prompted so little attention from scholars? And why does the legislative branch continue to play such a minor role in the Mexican policy process?[4]

The answers to these questions involve many variables, among the most important of which are historical precedent, the distribution of constitutional powers, the role of the executive branch (especially the presidency), the structure of the legislative system, the recruitment paths to power, the policymaking process, the function of elections, and institutional linkages to interest groups.

A Weak Legislative Heritage: The Historical Conspiracy

Mexico's 1917 Constitution establishes a republican system with a division of powers patterned intellectually and theoretically after that found in the United States. Mexico's political structure consists of three divisions: legislative, executive, and judicial. The legislative branch is bicameral in structure, and since the 1824 Constitution, Mexico's first postindependence document, it has been called the Congress. Congress is made up of the Chamber of Deputies (equivalent to the U.S. House of Representatives) and the Senate (originally called the Chamber of Senators).[5]

The similarities between the United States and Mexico are not confined to Congress's overall structure; they also include the manner in which both types of representatives are selected. Senators and deputies, until 1964, were chosen by direct popular vote. Deputies were selected on the basis of geographic districts, based on a roughly fixed population that was determined, as in the United States, by regular census data. Each deputy was selected for a three-year term. In Mexico, every other legislature is elected simultaneously with the president, who is selected to serve a six-year term with no possibility of reelection. Thus, the fifty-fourth legislature, elected coterminously with President Carlos Salinas in 1988, served until 1991. The present legislature, the fifty-fifth, will complete its term in 1994. In 1993, 300 deputies came from single-member districts. The three most populous states or entities, accounting for 32 percent of the seats in the Chamber of Deputies, are the Federal District (40 seats), México (34), and Veracruz (23).

Senators were selected for six-year terms until 1991, coterminous with a presidential term. In 1991, a new electoral law established staggered terms for senators; thus half who were elected in 1988 served only three years, from 1988 to 1991, whereas the remainder stayed on until 1994. A newly elected batch joined their previously elected colleagues for a six-year term from 1991 to 1997. Each state and the Federal District (somewhat similar to the District of Columbia in the United States, but far more significant politically, economically, and intellectually than the U.S. capital) is represented by two senators, for a total of 64.

The most important legal change introduced in the legislative branch since the 1970s is the proportional representation system, which exists alongside a single-member district system to yield a mixed electoral system, something like Germany's. Currently, 200 additional deputies are elected on the basis of a complex formula tied to each party's national vote totals for congressional candidates (bringing the total number of deputies to 500). In the 1960s and early 1970s, these deputies were known as party deputies, distinguishing them from single-member district types, but more recently they are identified as plurinominal deputies. Mexico is divided into a small number of broad, regional, plurinominal districts from which these individuals are selected. However, the deputies represent their parties, not a geographic area. Prior to 1988, the government party (the Institutional Revolutionary Party, or PRI) won overwhelming victories in single-member districts (typically 90 percent or higher), so no deputies represented the PRI among the proportional representation seats because that system compensates parties that do poorly in the single-member districts. That changed dramatically in 1988, when the PRI's fortunes at the voting booth took a radical downturn.[6]

Constitutional requirements for becoming a member of either chamber are fairly simple and unrestrictive. Essentially, an elected member must have been a natural born citizen and have reached age twenty-five for deputies or thirty-five for senators. In addition, each person has to either reside in the state for six months prior to the election (a weak barrier to carpetbaggers) or have been born in the state or entity he or she is representing. No individuals from the highest levels in the state or national executive branches or judicial branch, or at any level in the armed forces, can run without resigning their posts ninety days prior to the election.

Two structural features peculiar to Mexico's legislative branch are the selection of alternate senators and deputies and the reelection prohibition. According to William P. Tucker, the concept of the alternate legislator is Spanish in origin and can be found in all Mexican constitutions since 1824.[7] For each senator and deputy, therefore, an alternate is elected. This individual replaces his or her counterpart if for any reason (poor health, death, or appointment to another office) that individual cannot serve. Consequently, state governors in Mexico, unlike in the United States, are not given an opportunity to appoint temporary replacements to the national Congress. An alternate is free to hold any other post, and occasionally one encounters an alternate senator being elected a deputy three years into his tenure.

A more important feature having significant structural and policy-making consequences is the fact that legislative officials, at the state and national levels alike, cannot be reelected consecutively. This has little historical foundation in Mexico. During the long rein of Porfirio Díaz (1884–1911), numerous Mexicans served as senators or deputies from their home states, some as many as a half dozen times consecutively. Indeed, Díaz occasionally designated the same individual to run from two districts simultaneously, allowing his alternate to replace him in one of the posts. However, one of the basic precepts of the Mexican Revolution of 1910, and a firm postrevolutionary government motto, was that of no reelection.[8] This concept for the most part stemmed from presidential and gubernatorial longevity prior to 1910, not from that of legislators, who moved out of office more frequently. To many Mexicans of this era, abuse of power was synonymous with repetition in office. Thus at the executive branch level, a person who is mayor, governor, or president—even if designated only temporarily or as a substitute—can never hold that office again. Unlike so many other constitutional provisions in Mexico, this concept is firmly embedded in the political culture and has not been violated.[9] It was tested most recently in 1992 by the provisional governor of San Luis Potosí, who announced he would run in a gubernatorial race to be held the following year. Many political analysts believe his announcement was a trial run for his patron, President Carlos Salinas, to test the waters for presidential reelection. The suggestion was vociferously condemned, promptly disappearing from the political agenda.

In the case of legislators, the reelection restriction does not have such a strong basis in reality or myth. Following the Revolution of 1910 and the beginning of constitutionally elected presidents in 1920, numerous senators and legislators were elected consecutively, a practice continued until 1934, when the length of presidential terms was extended from four to six years, and deputy and senator terms from two to three years and four to six years, respectively. Interestingly, it can be argued that the high point of legislative independence and significant legislative debate since the Revolution occurred precisely during those years. This was also an era when many deputies and senators, veterans of the Revolution, attended sessions wearing sidearms.

Although the policymaking potential of Congress is strongly influenced by constitutional powers granted to and exercised by the executive branch, as well as by features of the electoral process, the consecutive reelection prohibition exercises a devastating impact on this branch of government. In the first place, one of the ways an individual can develop a successful political career is by holding legislative office. Many presidential contenders or top cabinet choices in the United States were serving in an elective or legislative office at the time of their designation, the majority of whom were from the U.S. Congress or state governorships, such as Jimmy Carter and Bill Clinton.

In Mexico, no president since 1920 has come from a career in the legislative branch.[10] Many presidents have served in the Chamber of Deputies early in their careers, but they did not come to the attention of incumbent presidents in their capacity as legislators. In recent decades, Mexican presidents have held no elective office.[11] Indeed, the last Mexican president to hold a congressional office was Gustavo Díaz Ordaz (1964–1970), who served as a deputy for his home state of Puebla from 1943 to 1946, almost two decades before he became president. This pattern, so unlike that in the United States, has serious implications for policymaking and personnel policies, which are strongly linked. Mexico's political leadership, as explained more fully later in this chapter, has been tied together institutionally and personally since the late 1920s. Given the dominance of a single political party (the PRI and its antecedents) and the presence of a single elite faction for so many decades, such structural prohibitions wield tremendous influence.

The legislative branch, as some of these historical and structural features imply, has very little prestige in Mexico. One of the reasons for this is that the legislature exercises little influence over decisionmaking. An institution whose reputation is modest does not attract the best political talents. Over the years, as the Mexican executive continued to exercise more influence and grow in size, it became apparent to most astute politicians that a career in the legislative branch would not lead to the upper echelons of the power structure, either nationally or at the state level (although more exceptions can be found in the latter).

Political recruitment paths also affect other forms of democratization. Democratization is typically measured by the competitiveness of the electoral process and the access of various groups and political organizations to decisionmaking power. It can also be measured by the characteristics of a polity's leadership, whether one considers their geographic, social, professional, or gender backgrounds. In Mexico, studies clearly demonstrate that political leaders, as in all political cultures, are disproportionately from selected backgrounds—in that sense, they are elites.[12] But these same studies also demonstrate that Mexican legislative members are less elite in terms of the above categories than members of the other two branches. Consequently, if the legislative branch is eliminated as a pool for future decisionmakers in the executive branch and if opposition parties cannot achieve national executive posts, then Mexico's leadership stems from a narrower, more homogeneous group of individuals than would otherwise be the case.

In fact, single-member districts guarantee a geographic diversity in

Congress by virtue of constitutional requirements; for example, only 16 percent of the current legislature is from the Federal District, compared with 52 percent of the top executive office holders.[13] As shown in Table 1.1, the legislative branch represents a larger percentage of working-class Mexicans (closer to the percentage in the overall population), and twice as many women find posts in the Senate and Chamber of Deputies than in the executive branch.[14]

Table 1.1   Comparison of Legislators and Executive Officials, 1989–1991

Background Variables	Legislators (%)	Executive Branch Officials (%)
Gender		
Female	12	5
Education		
Preparatory or less	21	2
Career Experience		
Political parties	78	41
Unions	54	16
Elective posts	99	7
Parents' Occupation		
Peasant	7	1
Laborer	3	1
Birthplace		
Federal District	13	51

Source: Diccionario Biográfico del Gobierno Mexicano (Mexico: Presidencia de la República, 1989), based on 1,113 officials and 560 legislators.

An individual who cannot serve repeatedly in a legislative post cannot develop name recognition, seniority, policy expertise, or constituency ties, all important characteristics of members of the U.S. Congress and elements that strengthen it vis-à-vis the executive branch, enhancing its role in the democratic process. In Mexico's legislative history, one does not find the type of conflict between legislative and executive branches characterizing the Chilean case, where each struggled to gain the upper hand in the policymaking arena.[15] In contrast, the weakness of Mexico's legislative branch in the policy arena makes it, from the governing elite's perspective, an ideal locus for channeling opposition representatives. In other words, it is no accident that opposition expansion has been confined nationally to the legislative branch, whereas on the state and local level the major opposition parties, the National Action Party (PAN) and the

Party of the Democratic Revolution (PRD), have achieved greater successes.

Elections represent another element defining Mexico's legislative process. It is especially relevant to understand their importance in determining political leadership. Mexico's electoral heritage is not akin to that found in a typical democracy, or for that matter, electoral processes in Latin America. Although other Latin American countries have suffered far more serious bouts of authoritarian rule, during which legislatures have been dispensed with altogether, South American countries have on previous occasions (sometimes for many years) witnessed highly competitive elections. Although Mexico does have a long history of opposition to its present leadership, extending well back to the 1940s, opposition has not been able to translate that experience into electoral strength or the winning of national offices, at least until 1988.[16]

Historically, the reason for this pattern is that elections in Mexico since 1929 have not functioned as a means of determining who will govern, but rather as a technique for mobilizing support for those who already governed. In other words, elections performed a legitimizing function, not one of distributing power.[17] Therefore, individuals who hoped to serve in the legislative branch found it more relevant to be members of the governing party; to have the ear of top party officials, influential governors, and (most important) the president; and to win their party's internal nomination process. In fact, until recently, whatever competition occurred took place *within* the PRI, among candidates and various interest groups. Obtaining the PRI nomination, until 1988, was essentially tantamount to being appointed to a post in a single-member district.

This pattern not only devalued the electoral process itself, but similarly adversely affected the composition of Congress. As Peter Smith suggests, the Senate in particular became a museum for political has-beens, a reward to those at the end of their careers or currently out of favor for a top executive post.[18]

The other explanation for the development of a dominant one-party system and the perfunctory role of elections stems strongly from Mexico's unique revolutionary political heritage. Although Uruguay developed a rather unusual approach for sharing power between two political factions, which was successful for many decades, Mexico's decade of civil violence defeated the opposition decisively and produced a broad-based, postrevolutionary elite who took on the name of the "Revolutionary Family."[19] This governing elite hoped through pragmatism and centralized control to prevent a repetition of political violence. The generations who fashioned Mexico's political system from the 1940s to the 1970s believed sincerely in eliminating violence at almost any cost.[20]

Legislative Policymaking: Democratic or Authoritarian?

In theory, the legislative branch, primarily the lower house, plays an important role in the decisionmaking process. In reality, however, legislative decisionmaking is affected by three broad features: the chamber's internal structure; the relationship between the party, legislative leadership, and the executive branch; and the electoral process.

Each chamber meets annually beginning in September and normally remains in session until January. Both the Senate and the Chamber of Deputies designate a president and vice-president for each month they are in session. These individuals handle parliamentary aspects of the meetings. In reality, the most important member of each chamber is the equivalent of a majority leader. Naturally, since 1929, the majority leader has been a member of the government party. Theoretically, the majority leader is selected by the members of each chamber. In reality, he or she is designated by the Mexican president.[21] This is important for two reasons. First, it establishes both symbolically and in reality the subordination of the legislative branch to the executive branch. Second, the legislative branch lacks internal democracy within the majority party, as distinct from excluding opposition parties from legislative decisionmaking.

Both houses, similar to the U.S. Congress, have a long-established committee system. Both standing and special committees exist, and they are quite numerous, many compatible in scope to those found in the United States. Unlike the U.S. Congress, however, congressional committees do not wield comparable power. In the first place, one of the features that strengthens the legislative branch and makes it a competitor to the executive branch in the policymaking process is its ability to provide its own expertise and information. In the United States, Congress makes use of extensive, highly skilled aides and the Library of Congress research staff. In Mexico, most deputies and senators have only several employees, typically secretaries. Therefore, Mexican legislators rely on the executive branch for information, interpretations, and policy recommendations rather than on their own or independent sources.

Some deputies and senators develop personal expertise. Though it is true that such individuals are often members of or even chair committees where their expertise is useful, they are unable to take full advantage of their skills and, more important, establish public recognition of their expertise because of the reelection prohibition. Opposition party members are also assigned to appropriate committees, but because they are in the minority, they do not chair committees. Individuals who direct important legislative finance committees, for example, do not receive media recognition, nor do they develop a political following. Legislators' staffing budgets are so small that the legislators lack the means of providing any patronage to potential supporters.

Typically, the president introduces a bill in the legislative system. Theoretically, individual members of state legislatures can present a bill to Congress, but in fact almost all legislation is initiated by the executive. Bills can be introduced into either chamber, although those dealing with fiscal matters must originate in the Chamber of Deputies. During the last three administrations, since 1976, the percentage of executive-initiated legislation has actually increased, reaching over 90 percent in the first three years of Salinas's administration.

To be passed in the Chamber of Deputies, a bill must receive a simple majority, easily within reach of the government party. The only legislature for which the government party was in danger of losing its quorum was in the 1988–1991 session, when the PRI maintained a bare majority of seats. The president may veto a bill in whole or in part, but because both chambers have always been controlled by the government party, because party nominations are influenced by the incumbent president, and because the president designates congressional leadership, little need exists for the veto power to be exercised.

Perhaps the most important committee in the Mexican legislative system is the Gran Comisión (Great Committee) in each chamber, consisting of one member from each state. Typically, the individual selected has prior experience in either body or is currently in favor with the leadership. This committee makes appointments to each chamber's standing and special committees.[22] The most peculiar feature of Congress's internal structure is the Permanent Committee. This committee consists of fifteen deputies and fourteen senators who are appointed when the regular session terminates; it functions when both chambers are in recess. William Tucker notes that the Constitution gives the committee some specified and quite extraordinary powers, nearly all of which are granted to the Congress generally. However, unlike in the Congress, no minority party legislators are members of the Permanent Committee, which often functions as a substitute Congress for more than half a year.[23]

One of the ways in which the legislative branch contributes to the decentralization of authority and establishes channels for articulating views and influencing decisionmaking is through its ties with interest groups. A quick study of the Mexican legislature would readily reveal that unlike in other Latin American countries, interest groups are not represented before the chamber. In fact, lobbyists do not exist in Mexican legislative circles. Interest group organizations, where they do exist, direct their lobbying efforts toward the executive branch, to cabinet and subcabinet officials in those agencies having responsibility for their interests.[24] Thus, not only have interest groups not been well developed in Mexico, but they operate on only one level. Moreover, interest groups are able to function in much greater secrecy vis-à-vis the executive branch than if they were to operate amongst competing parties in both congressional chambers.

One explanation for the weak interest group functions in Mexico is the establishment of a corporatist system. Under President Lázaro Cárdenas (1934–1940), the state enhanced its corporatist structure, not only initiating specific interest organizations such as national business groups, but also bringing many interest groups (particularly agrarian, labor, and professional) under the umbrella of the government party.[25] In effect, party membership could be achieved only through membership in one of the umbrella organizations. This party membership statute was not changed until 1992. Most politicians, for example, and eventually most legislators, were members of the amorphous popular sector, the National Confederation of Popular Organizations (CNOP), an umbrella confederation for bureaucrats and teachers unions and other professional groups, such as doctors, lawyers, economists, etc.

The implications of corporatism for Mexico's legislative branch are significant. Given the PRI's dominance, the party conceptualized itself as representing most interest groups—organizations already incorporated into its own structure. Therefore, little need existed for organizations to pressure legislators because their own members were automatically incorporated into the party and into the legislative structure. The national party leadership, represented by the National Executive Committee, included secretaries for each of the three pillars of the party corporatist structure: labor, agrarian, and popular. Typically, the top leaders of the most influential organizations of these three sectors—the Confederation of Mexican Workers (CTM), the Confederación Nacional Campesina (CNC), and the CNOP—were themselves appointed to these posts. In turn, each of these secretaries was nominated by the party and elected in a "safe" district to the Chamber of Deputies or Senate.[26]

A built-in linkage exists among party leadership, legislative leadership, and the presidency in Mexico. In Latin American countries, corporatist influences can also be found. But in those countries, which have seen numerous parties competing for power, various parties represent these interests. For example, in Chile the Communist Party, the Social Democratic Party, and the Christian Democratic Party all had affiliated labor unions. In Mexico, however, weak development of both nationally based parties, as well as competing interest organizations (especially among organized labor), discouraged strong interest group associations with other political parties, especially prior to 1985.

The other structural feature that distinguishes Mexico's political system from all other Latin American countries except Costa Rica is the military's subordination to civilian control. In Mexico, given the fact that the legislative branch was not a channel to the decisionmaking process, political parties did not form alliances with disaffected military officers. Mexico's revolutionary, military leadership actually established the government party, creating the political elite and transferring the party to civilian control in 1946.[27] Indeed, the lack of military subordination to civilian leadership elsewhere in Latin America, as well as the military's direct involvement in partisan politics, explains much of the instability, authoritarianism, and intervention found in the region.

One of the interesting consequences of Mexico's legislative structure and its indirect personnel ties to the executive branch is that little public discussion exists about policy decisions, including budget matters. Generally, budget allocations in Latin American countries and in the United States receive intensive media attention. Almost no discussion of these decisions occurs in Mexico. For example, the defense budget, hotly debated in the United States, is entirely unknown in Mexican circles, even among the most highly educated.[28]

One of the peculiarities of Mexico's legislative process, given the relationship between the two branches of government, is the ease with which the Constitution can be, and is, amended. The presidency has used this power to legitimize controversial policy issues. Constitutional change requires only a two-thirds majority. One of the most recent policy controversies concerned proposed legislation to revise constitutional articles on church-state relations and the political activities of religious officials, primarily the Catholic Church.

The legislative leadership assigned the proposed changes to a small group of deputies knowledgeable about constitutional and political implications. According to legislative procedure, this committee should have recommended a bill. The executive agency that is most informed about church-state issues in Mexico and is required to enforce established constitutional restrictions is the Secretariat of Government. Officials of this agency have had years of experience dealing with problems involving these specific constitutional provisions. In fact, however, the highly controversial legislation proposed by the Chamber of Deputies came not from the special committee, nor in consultation with the most knowledgeable and involved executive agency, but from the presidency, which under President Salinas's chief adviser, José Córdoba, appointed its own experts to make the final recommendations.[29]

Legislative Democratization: Leader or Follower?

The view presented of legislative change and democratization in Mexico thus far is discouraging. However, there are some changes taking place, and some of them may have long-term consequences. These consequences may be far more durable than those found in some of the other countries under study in this book; Mexico is evolving gradually, rather than fluctuating wildly between competitive elections and acrimonious legislative debate versus authoritarian repression and declaration of emergency powers. Democratization influences are not reintroducing elections to Mexico or establishing them for the first time in recent memory, as is true elsewhere in Latin America; instead they are modifying the process and purpose of elections.

Mexico's leadership has always understood the importance of appearances and of pragmatic flexibility in dealing with political opponents. Up through 1993 that leadership never seriously considered giving up power, but prior to 1988 it believed itself to be politically invincible on the *national* level. Consequently, as pressures for democratization increased in the 1970s, Mexico's leadership devised a means to restore more vitality to the electoral process, and consequently to the Congress, where the results would be most visible.

In 1977, the passage of the Federal Law of Political Organizations and Electoral Processes (LFOPPE) added 100 plurinominal deputies to the 300 deputies elected by majority districts (though this number was later revised). Because the PRI did not receive any of these additional seats under the proportional representation formula, in effect a minimum of 25 percent of the seats were allocated to the opposition, in addition to whatever remaining seats they might be able to win in single-member districts.

The data in Table 1.2 illustrate the proportional representation system's impact on the legislative branch. In 1979, the first year after the new plurinominal system went into effect, the PRI controlled 296 seats and the opposition 104. That pattern remained essentially unchanged through 1985, although the PRI gave up seven additional single-member districts. Nevertheless, the government controlled 72 percent of all seats, an overwhelming majority. However, what these figures fail to show is that support for the government party, even by its own tainted official tallies, was declining rapidly. Although the PRI continued to win single-member districts, the percentage of its victory narrowed in a third of those districts, particularly in the Federal District, Guadalajara, Ciudad Juárez, and the state of México. There, though the party controlled 72 percent of the seats in the Chamber of Deputies in the 1985–1988 legislature, its legislative candidates received only 65 percent of the vote (see Table 1.3). This situation, along with deplorable economic conditions and the candidacy of Cuauthémoc Cárdenas, a politician with considerable name recognition and supporters, laid the groundwork for the radical departure in opposition strength in the 1988 presidential and congressional elections.

Table 1.2   Seats in the Chamber of Deputies by Party, 1949–1991

Legislature	PRI	PAN	PPS	PARM	PDM	PSUM	PST	PRT	PMT	PRD	PFCRN
1949	142	4	1	—	—	—	—	—	—	—	—
1952a	152	5	2	—	—	—	—	—	—	—	—
1955	155	6	1	—	—	—	—	—	—	—	—
1958a	153	6	1	1	—	—	—	—	—	—	—
1961	172	5	1	—	—	—	—	—	—	—	—
1964	175	2	1	—	—	—	—	—	—	—	—
Party	—	18	9	5	—	—	—	—	—	—	—
1967	177	1	0	0	—	—	—	—	—	—	—
Party	—	19	10	5	—	—	—	—	—	—	—
1970	178	0	0	0	—	—	—	—	—	—	—
Party	—	20	10	5	—	—	—	—	—	—	—
1973	189	4	—	1	—	—	—	—	—	—	—
Party	—	21	10	6	—	—	—	—	—	—	—
1976	195	—	—	2	—	—	—	—	—	—	—
Party	—	20	12	9	—	—	—	—	—	—	—
1979	296	4	—	—	—	—	—	—	—	—	—
Plurin.	—	39	11	12	10	18	10	—	—	—	—
1982	299	1	—	—	—	—	—	—	—	—	—
Plurin.	—	50	10	0	12	17	11	—	—	—	—
1985	289	9	—	2	—	—	—	—	—	—	—
Plurin.	—	32	11	9	12	12	12	6	6	—	—
1988	233	38	3	6	—	—	—	—	—	—	1
Plurin.	27	63	32	25	—	—	—	—	—	38	34
1991	290	10	—	—	—	—	—	—	—	—	—
Plurin.	31	80	12	14	—	—	—	—	—	40	23

Source: Adapted from Héctor Zamitiz and Carlos Hernández, "La Composición Política de la Camara de Diputados, 1949–1989," *Revista de Ciencias Politicas y Sociales,* Vol. 36, No. 139 (January–March, 1990), pp. 97–108.
Note: a. Three other seats were won by members of the Federation of Popular Mexican Parties and the Mexican Nationalist Party.

Table 1.3   Percentages of Votes for Major Mexican Parties for National Legislators, 1961–1991

Election	Parties										
	PRI	PAN	PPS	PARM	PDM	PSUM	PST	PRT	PMT	PRD	PFCRN
1961	90.2	7.6	1.0	0.5	—	—	—	—	—	—	—
1964	86.3	11.5	1.4	0.7	—	—	—	—	—	—	—
1967	83.3	12.4	2.8	1.3	—	—	—	—	—	—	—
1970	80.1	13.9	1.4	0.8	—	—	—	—	—	—	—
1973	69.7	14.7	3.6	1.9	—	—	—	—	—	—	—
1976	80.1	8.5	3.0	2.5	—	—	—	—	—	—	—
1979	69.7	10.8	2.6	1.8	2.1	4.9	2.7	—	—	—	—
1982	69.3	17.5	1.9	1.4	2.2	4.4	1.8	1.3	—	—	—
1985	65.0	15.5	2.0	1.7	2.7	3.2	2.5	1.3	1.5	—	—
1988	50.4	17.1	9.2	6.1	0.4	—	—	0.2	—	—	9.4
1991	61.4	17.7	1.8	2.1	1.1	—	—	0.6	—	8.3	4.4

Source: Adapted from Delal Baer, "The 1991 Mexican Midterm Elections," Center for Strategic and International Studies, Latin American Election Study Series, Georgetown University, Washington, D.C., October 1, 1991, p. 31.

In 1986, the government revised the electoral law again, this time doubling plurinominal deputies to 200 and leaving single-member districts unchanged at 300. The 1986 revision also modified Article 54 of the law, giving the majority party access to proportional representation (PR) seats if its total dropped below that of a simple majority (251), which would place the party in jeopardy of losing control over the Chamber of Deputies.[30] At the stroke of a pen, this legislation expanded opposition from 25 to 40 percent. Earlier, in 1983, Article 115 of the Constitution was reformed to extend the PR concept to state legislatures and municipal city councils.

The effect of the LFOPPE and its subsequent revisions can be seen from both Tables 1.2 and 1.3. As Silvia Gómez Tagle concludes, "In spite of everything, the possibility of winning elections through the PR system stimulated competition and the development of opposition parties, especially when the system began to be extended to state congressional and municipal elections."[31] However, the law did have another positive effect. A party's legal recognition would be determined by its ability to obtain 1.5 percent of the vote. Although this opened up the party process to some new, radical left parties, other parties previously recognized by the government could not sustain even this minimal support and were automatically dropped from the ballot.

The 1988 election is a benchmark in terms of Mexican electoral history and as a measure of democratization within the electoral process and in the legislative branch. Interestingly, the pressure for democratization came from within the party leadership. A group designating itself as the Democratic Current attempted to get the party to commit to changing the electoral process—essentially to allow clean elections to determine the political fortunes of the respective parties. When the group failed in 1987, its leading members, including Cuauthémoc Cárdenas (son of President Cárdenas) and Porfirio Muñoz Ledo (a former PRI president) bolted from the party and established their own electoral front. Some of the PRI's minority allies joined the Cárdenas faction, as did other parties on the left (the PPS, PFCRN, PST, and PMS). Four of the eight parties on the 1988 ballot supported the younger Cárdenas's candidacy.[32]

It is clear that the PRI committed widespread fraud to sustain its electoral victory in 1988, how extensive we will never know. Regardless of whether Cuauthémoc Cárdenas actually won the 1988 elections, PRI support was devastated. The impact on the legislative branch was extraordinary. First, Congress must approve election results, thereby determining Carlos Salinas's victory. Second, although the PRI resorted to the 1986 reforms to obtain a simple majority in the Chamber of Deputies in 1988, it obtained only 233 victories in single-member districts, so it did not have sufficient votes to win approval of constitutional reforms, a technique long used to legitimize important or controversial legislation. Third, for the first time, the PRI was forced to work out a compromise with an opposition party in order to obtain important legislation. It chose to develop a legislative alliance with the PAN, which although strongly opposed to the PRI's stance on political democratization, favored Salinas's strategy on free trade and economic privatization.

Fourth, and perhaps most important, the locus of Mexican democratic change from 1988 to 1991 became the legislative branch. Salinas came into office with little or no legitimacy. Given the PRI's poor showing in the elections and the newly created pressures from opposition parties, the presidency was forced to negotiate still another political reform, this time with the PAN's collaboration. Although the 1990 Federal Code of Electoral Institutions and Procedures (COFIPE) contains many significant changes, the most important for the legislative branch specifically is the so-called governability clause. The PRI, recognizing its own weakness, altered Article 51 of the Mexican Constitution a second time, incorporating the principle that any party winning over 35 percent of the vote will be given the necessary plurinominal seats to achieve a simple majority. In other words, although opposition parties collectively might win as much as 65 percent of the votes, the PRI could still sustain a majority in the Chamber of Deputies.

Although the law's supporters claim that opposition parties received other benefits positively affecting voter registration and ballot counting, many analysts believe COFIPE is a setback for democratization and for opposition parties. Furthermore, it reduced the pressure on the PRI, changing the focus away from the legislative branch to the electoral arena itself. The results of the 1991 election reinforced this pessimistic interpretation (see Table 1.4)

Table 1.4   Representation in the Legislative Branch, 1991–1994

Party	District Seats	Deputies Party Seats	Total	Senators
PRI	290	31	321	61
PAN	10	80	90	1
PRD	0	40	40	2
PFCRN	0	23	23	0
PARM	0	14	14	0
PPS	0	12	12	0
Totals	300	200	500	64

Source: Adapted from *The Other Side of Mexico,* No. 22, July–August 1991, p. 4.
Note: The other parties (the PDM, PSUM, PST, PRT, and PMT) did not win 1.5 percent of the vote and so lost their national registration.

Basically, the legislative pattern suggested in Table 1.4, compared with the data in Tables 1.2 and 1.3, shows a return to the pre-1988 electoral results, in which the PRI obtained about 290 of the 300 single-member district seats; but the PRI also gained an additional increment of plurinominal deputies for each percentage of the vote beyond 35 percent.

During the intervening legislature (1988–1991), the PRI, PAN, and PRD (Cuauthémoc Cárdenas's newly formed party after 1988) were forced to use those skills found in any functioning democracy: compromise and negotiation. Although such behavior has not disappeared altogether, the level, tone, and importance of it have declined since 1991. In contrast, an internal pressure for democratic change continues to persist within the legislature. According to many deputies, there have been complaints to the majority leader about the undemocratic determination of legislative assignments and leadership contrary to congressional statutes.

The persistence of plurinominal representation on the national and state levels assigns legislative bodies in Mexico an important role in democratization. Although the achievements have as yet been minimal, especially on the policymaking level, they are having an effect. The government party is being forced to select more skillful politicians, and is reversing (somewhat) the exclusive trend of the technocrats. Among the three leading contenders for the PRI presidential nomination in 1993, two had extensive political skills. The first, Donaldo Colosio, was the first party chair and former deputy to be in contention in many years. The second, Manuel Camacho, who deals with powerful interest groups daily as the head of the administrative agency of the Federal District, is a masterful politician. Finally, Fernando Ortiz Arana, Salinas's majority leader in the 1991–1994 Chamber of Deputies, was selected in 1993 to become president of the PRI, allegedly because of skills he demonstrated negotiating with the PAN and PRD. Furthermore, demands for elective representation increased dramatically in the Federal District, which accounts for nearly a fifth of the population but has no elective governor. The government created the Assembly of the Federal District, similar to a state legislature, and demands for increasing its policymaking influence grew dramatically in 1993.[33]

Potentially, the most important change for the legislative process was introduced by Ernesto Zedillo, the successful PRI candidate for the presidency, several months before taking office on December 1, 1994. Zedillo promised to separate his party from the government, and specifically, to permit the party, not the incumbent president, to choose the party's presidential candidate. Shortly after the August presidential elections, in which his party again won a majority of the seats in the legislative branch, PRI delegates began selecting candidates for local and state elections, including gubernatorial candidates in Guanajuato and Jalisco, a choice historically reserved for Mexican presidents. If Zedillo is successful in implementing this candidate selection process, and applying it as well to congressional nominations for the 1997 elections, then a major source of the executive branch's control over the legislative bodies will be broken, and legislators, who are members of the president's party, will have greater independence.

The intertwining of electoral reforms, legislative representation, and democratization has had some impact on Mexico. Although not reaching the pace of reforms found elsewhere in the region, Mexico is not likely to discard such changes altogether, but rather to build slowly and firmly the foundation for a democratic polity.

Notes

1. Alan Angel, et al., "Latin America," in *Electioneering, A Comparative Study of Continuity and Change,* ed. by David Butler and Austin Ranney (Oxford: Clarendon Press, 1992).

2. For a useful discussion of conceptualizing democracy, see Terry Lynn Karl, "Dilemmas of Democratization in Latin America," *Comparative Politics,* Vol. 23 (October 1990), pp. 2–3.

3. The most useful overview I have seen of democratization and its conceptualization is John Markoff, "Historical Waves of Democratization and Latin America in the 1990s," in *Deepening Democracy and Representation in Latin America,* ed. by Kurt von Mettenheim and James Malloy (Pittsburgh: University of Pittsburgh Press, forthcoming).

4. The only previous study of Latin American legislatures, that by Weston Agor (ed.), *Latin American Legislatures: Their Role and Influence* (New York: Praeger, 1971), ignores the Mexican case altogether.

5. William P. Tucker, *Mexican Government Today* (Minneapolis: University of Minnesota Press, 1954), p. 91.

6. For an excellent history of how this evolved, see Silvia Gómez Tagle, "Electoral Reform and the Party System, 1977–90," in *Mexico, Dilemmas of Transition,* ed. by Neil Harvey (London: Institute of Latin American Studies, University of London, 1993), pp. 64–90.

7. William P. Tucker, *Mexican Government Today,* p. 92.

8. Francisco I. Madero, who contested Porfirio Díaz in the 1910 presidential elections, popularized this motto in his book *La sucesión presidencial en 1910* (San Pedro: Coahuila, 1908). For many years after 1920, up through the early 1970s, government correspondence included a stamped imprint below official signatures stating "Effective Suffrage and No Reelection."

9. The last time an attempt was made to alter this pattern occurred in 1928, when ex-president Alvaro Obregón (1920–1924) persuaded his supporters in Congress to amend the Constitution, allowing for nonconsecutive reelection. Obregón ran, was elected president in 1928, but was assassinated before taking office. The constitutional provision on reelection was restored to its original state.

10. An informal rule of Mexican politics is that the contender for the PRI presidential nomination must come directly from the cabinet. That person is designated by the incumbent president. Positions in certain cabinets, notably national defense, government, treasury, and planning and budgeting, have produced most of the successful aspirants. For a detailed discussion of the evolution of these qualities, see my "Mexican Presidential Pre-candidates, Changes and Portents for the Future," *Polity,* Vol. 6 (Summer 1984), pp. 588–605.

11. It is increasingly rare among cabinet members, too, and because the cabinet provides the pool for presidential nominees from the PRI, its composition determines presidential qualities. For example, in Miguel de la Madrid's initial cabinet (1982–1988), only one figure had been in the Congress.

12. Peter H. Smith, *Labyrinths of Power: Political Recruitment in Twentieth Century Mexico* (Princeton, New Jersey: Princeton University Press, 1979); and Roderic Ai Camp, *Mexico's Leaders: Their Education and Recruitment* (Tucson: University of Arizona Press, 1980).

13. *Diccionario Biográfico del Gobierno Mexicano* (Mexico: Presidencia de la República, 1992), pp. 1043, 1051.

14. Roderic Ai Camp, "Modernization and Recruitment: The Case of Mexico," unpublished manuscript, 1993.

15. Federico Gil, *The Political System of Chile* (Boston: Houghton Mifflin, 1966).

16. See my "Mexico's 1988 Elections: A Turning Point for Its Political Development and Foreign Relations," in *Sucesión Presidencial: The 1988 Mexican Presidential Elections*, ed. by Edgar W. Butler and Jorge A. Bustamante (Boulder: Westview, 1990), pp. 104–108.

17. I develop this argument, as well as its relationship to democratization, in considerable detail in "Battling for the Voter: Elections, Parties and Democracy in Mexico," in *Deepening Democracy and Representation in Latin America*, ed. by Kurt von Metenheim and James Malloy (Pittsburgh: University of Pittsburgh Press, forthcoming).

18. Peter H. Smith, *Labyrinths of Power,* p. 226.

19. See Martin Weinstein, *Uruguay: The Politics of Failure* (Westport: Greenwood Press, 1975), for insightful background to this procedure.

20. See statements by contemporaries of President Miguel Alemán (1946–1952) in my *The Making of a Government: Political Leaders in Modern Mexico* (Tucson: University of Arizona Press, 1984), p. 42ff.

21. For example, President Salinas selected Gonzalo Martínez Corbalá as his majority leader, the man he later selected to handle an extremely delicate political situation in the state of San Luis Potosí. Martínez Corbalá had given the president his first political position as an aide in a Federal District party post.

22. The most detailed description of the committee system and the bill process is Rodolfo de la Garza, "The Mexican Chamber of Deputies and the Mexican Political System," unpublished Ph.D. diss., University of Arizona, 1972.

23. In the 1988–1991 Senate, two members were from the PRD because that party captured both Senate seats in two states (the Federal District and Michoacán).

24. For some excellent case studies of policy decisions, see Susan Kaufman Purcell, *The Mexican Profit-Sharing Decision: Politics in an Authoritarian Regime* (Berkeley: University of California Press, 1975); and Merilee Grindle, *Bureaucrats, Politicians, and Peasants in Mexico: A Case Study in Public Policy* (Berkeley: University of California Press, 1977).

25. A detailed explanation of this corporatist structure can be found in Ruth Berins Collier, *The Contradictory Alliance: State-Labor Relations and Regime Change in Mexico* (Berkeley: International and Area Studies, University of California, 1992), Chapter 2.

26. The ability of the party to continue operating in an increasingly open and democratic environment has been carefully analyzed in John J. Bailey, *Governing Mexico: The Statecraft of Crisis Management* (New York: St. Martin's Press, 1988).

27. I provide a detailed history of this peculiar evolution and its consequences for Mexican politics, as well as the linkages between the military and politics, in *Generals in the Palacio: The Military in Modern Mexico* (New York: Oxford University Press, 1992).

28. Roderic Ai Camp, *Generals in the Palacio,* p. 50.

29. Interviews in Mexico City with a member of the Chamber of Deputies committee, and a top official of the Secretariat of Government, August 1992.

30. Prior to 1986, only parties obtaining fewer than twenty single-member districts could have proportional representation deputies.

31. Silvia Gómez Tagle, "Electoral Reform and the Party System," p. 70.

32. For excellent background on the succession process, see Peter H. Smith, "The 1988 Presidential Succession in Historical Perspective," in *Mexico's Alternative Political Futures,* ed. by Wayne Cornelius, et al. (La Jolla: United States–Mexico Studies Center, UCSD, 1989), p. 399ff.

33. A recent poll by Miguel Basáñez, published in *Excélsior,* concluded that 81 percent of Federal District residents wanted to elect their own mayor. February 27, 1993, p. 1.

2

The Salvadoran
National Legislature

José Z. Garcia

Historical Background: Traditional Legislative Functions

In 1841, during a moment of regional turmoil, General Francisco Malespin, commander of the armed forces of El Salvador, stormed into the office of President Juan Lindo and said, "I won't leave here until you promise to create a national university." In spite of Lindo's opposition, Malespin was able to pressure the Constituent Assembly (which had legislative powers) to pass a decree establishing the university on February 16, 1841, but a few months later Lindo ordered the project aborted for lack of funds. "I would rather sell my epaulets than see this school closed," Malespin is said to have remarked, forcing Lindo to save the institution.[1]

More than a century and a half later, in 1983, during another moment of regional turmoil, a weak president was unable to persuade enough members of El Salvador's thirteenth Constituent Assembly (which had legislative powers) to vote for a proposal on agrarian reform. Once again, a general responding to pressure from abroad (in this case the U.S. government) turned the tide. General Eugenio Vides Casanova, the minister of defense, jumped into a jeep, drove to the legislative palace, and pressured the two or three deputies he needed to pass the legislation. Again the legislative body deferred to the wishes of informal but consequential military power.

These two anecdotes reveal a good deal about the relationship between the legislature, the armed forces, and presidential power in El Salvador for the past 150 years. During the nineteenth century the presidency was weak, and parties organized at local and regional levels more for war with each other than for elections or governing. In the absence of a national army, presidents who did not have personal or regional armies to back them were vulnerable; when local opposition

37

to Lindo surfaced, for example, he promptly resigned the presidency.[2] During the five years that Malespin dominated Salvadoran politics, eight men (including Malespin himself, but only for a few months) were named chief of state.[3] Although the presidency strengthened during the twentieth century, it has remained relatively weak during periods of crisis, such as the civil war of the 1980s.

Moreover, politics in El Salvador has both local and regional tendencies. Malespin dominated El Salvador as a surrogate for Guatemalan general Rafael Carrera, a Conservative whose influence stretched over a good portion of Central America for several years after he defeated Francisco Morazan in 1840. Malespin was killed in 1846. His head was severed and placed in a birdcage, which was hung from a lamppost just outside San Salvador.[4] This occurred during fighting against a Liberal rebellion that had broken out in Nicaragua, precipitating a five-year return of Liberals to power in El Salvador. Conservatives and Liberals fought regionally and locally until the late nineteenth century, when liberalism finally triumphed throughout the isthmus. In the 1980s, during a regional crisis caused in part by the widespread collapse of liberalism, regional politics again affected internal power relations.

Finally, though clearly affected by local and regional currents, the legislature was too weak to affect them. The government budget in 1844 was only 118,713 pesos,[5] hardly enough to build more than a few schools and roads each year. In the Malespin-Lindo example above, when cross-pressured by local and regional demands, the legislature chose to support the informal but consequential power of Malespin rather than the formal but less potent authority of Lindo, a typical response by a legislature that would survive as an institution during many difficult times by making just such choices. Opposition legislators could suddenly find themselves in exile for years at a time. In 1983 the legislature's deference to military power had longstanding precedence.

As regional influences waned during most of the twentieth century, the presidency acquired more power. As coffee taxes enriched the coffers of the treasury, government budgets expanded greatly, broadening the scope of government. But the armed forces continued to dominate as a political actor, and the legislature, although it continued to meet annually for a few days to approve budgets and gossip about current events, did not escape the subordinate role it played during the formative years of national life. And when regimes in Central America faced a serious regional challenge to traditional rule during the 1980s, many of the relationships implied in the first anecdote still prevailed in El Salvador. Legislatures, in short, have played secondary roles in politics, behind armies, oligarchies, dictators, and parties. In El Salvador they have done little more than paint a patina of legitimacy to decisions already made in other arenas, including theaters of war.

During the last decade, efforts have been made to constitute a regime in which the armed forces would play a subordinate role and elections would choose a representative legislature that, in theory at least, would have powerful capabilities. With an internationally supervised peace process well in place, and with the political left willing or able for the first time since 1932 to participate freely in legislative elections, there is some anticipation that the legislature will be able to represent the interests of all organized sectors of Salvadoran society. Is there enough evidence available to determine whether the role of the legislature has changed? What can be expected of the legislature in this new effort to constitute a political regime? The major conclusion in this chapter is that although the legislature may improve its institutional capacity to perform constituent services, it is unlikely to develop much autonomy in relation to other political institutions.

The Current Legislature

The current political system in El Salvador was constituted in 1982 with the election of an assembly empowered to write a new constitution; presidential and legislative elections followed, and three civilian presidents have been elected since 1984. The previous regime had collapsed in 1979, precipitating a civil war that was well on its way in 1982 to being won by armed Marxist guerrilla rebels. Most of the old regime's backers had fled the country, leaving only a skeleton government composed of the Christian Democratic Party (not a backer of the old regime, but also not in favor of Marxist victory) and the armed forces, split among various groups who agreed only that the old regime was finished and that the guerrillas must be stopped.

Because the collapse in 1979 was largely a product of the old regime's rapid and widespread loss of legitimacy (caused by fraudulent elections, increasing exclusion, draconian repression, and economic mismanagement), the surviving government desperately needed to inflate itself with enough legitimacy to survive in an extremely hostile environment. The international news media, various governments in the region, global human rights and church groups, and many sectors of the politically relevant population of El Salvador were either predicting or advocating a Sandinista-style victory for the guerrillas. Fearful of such prospects, the Reagan administration devised a plan that would offer the "carrot" of procedural and substantive reform to legitimize the government while providing the "stick" of military assistance.

U.S. military assistance thus became, in the language of low-intensity conflict, an umbrella against a Marxist victory, under which a new, more popular regime would constitute itself and acquire enough legitimacy at home and abroad to survive. Elections, a new legislature, and other trappings of democratic governance were not the only legitimizing features of this project. Agrarian reform, judicial reform, banking reform, and police reform were also viewed as issues that would help legitimize the government's intentions at a symbolic level distinct from that of procedural democracy. These were duly decreed and executed, with enormous amounts of foreign assistance.

The first four elected legislatures (1982, 1985, 1988, and 1991) did not accurately reflect national ideological distributions because the left did not participate in the first three elections and only minimally in the fourth. Indeed, the left opposed the very notion of elections, deeming them as constituting one of the symbols and weapons being used to legitimize a regime they hoped to destroy. Only in 1994, after peace accords were signed under the supervision of the United Nations, did all organized parties participate in elections. During the course of the civil war, then, the legislature represented only the center-right and extreme right of the political spectrum. Like their predecessors 150 years before, legislators tended to wait for cues concerning expected behavior—in this case from the armed forces, government officials, the U.S. embassy, a few party leaders, and well-organized interest groups.

In the beginning, although ideologically opposed to the reforms undertaken by the government headed by Christian Democrat Napoleon Duarte, the extreme right tended to capitulate to major reforms when the U.S. government sent cues that these were necessary to convince the U.S. Congress to continue sending military and economic assistance. The legislature, although dominated by the extreme right, thereby came to reflect the views of the center or center-right. By the late 1980s, when it became clear the guerrillas had no chance of winning and the Duarte government had discredited itself with corruption and economic stagnation (some of which was caused by the guerrilla campaign against the economy), the extreme right organized more forcefully and elected a president and legislature dominated by its own partisans. The reformist cast to the government ceased.

The Legislature's Role in the Peace Process

El Salvador experienced a unique end to its civil war in that the United Nations participated in the negotiations and agreements to end the war and has helped supervise the peace. The agreements included the creation of several institutions designed to assist in the gradual incorporation of the guerrillas into the civic life of the regime. A commission for the consolidation of peace (known as COPAZ) was formed, with civilians representing all parties in the legislature to verify compliance with the peace agreements. One of its tasks was to supervise the resolution of land disputes between those who hold title to land in areas affected by civil war and those now occupying the land. A truth commission composed of foreign leaders was appointed to investigate and reveal the facts in unresolved cases concerning human rights abuses committed by the combatants on both sides. An ad hoc commission was also appointed to evaluate and supervise a host of changes contemplated for the armed forces.[6]

What is perhaps most striking about the peace agreements is that major political parties were formally consulted in all aspects of the dialogue while it was taking place; it fell upon the legislature to formalize what had already been agreed to. For example, in a September 1990 agreement reached by an interparty dialogue commission, political parties agreed with the Faribundo Marti Front for National Liberation (FMLN) and the government to revise the election rules governing the March 1991 legislative and municipal elections. These changes expanded the size of the legislative assembly from sixty to eighty-four seats, a measure deemed essential to securing participation by the left. Political parties also participated in the discussions leading to the creation of the truth commission and thwarted efforts by the FMLN to change constitutional amendment procedures. The legislature cooperated fully in enacting legislation to make these changes with little, if any, debate.

The national legislature, then, did not participate directly in peace discussions, even though individual members did (because political parties were included). And after the peace agreements went into effect in 1992, the legislature has had to share the stage temporarily with COPAZ, a body in which members of political parties meet with government officials and guerrillas to propose legislation to foster the peace process. These developments suggest that major actors on both sides of the civil war believed the legislature's capabilities and stature were insufficient to warrant direct participation in the negotiations; this belief represents a tacit commentary on the legislature's prominence in Salvadoran political affairs and a confirmation of the long-held historical notion in El Salvador that the legislature *reflects* political power rather than creating or possessing it.

Organization of the Legislative Assembly

The Constituent Assembly, whose task it was to draft the 1983 Constitution, created a legislature of sixty persons, amended in 1990 to eighty-four persons. Legislative elections are distinct from presidential and municipal elections—even when all the elections are held on the same date; that is, separate lists enable voters to select different parties for the legislature and president. Party composition in the legislature is determined through a system of proportional representation.

The leadership consists of one president, three vice-presidents, five secretaries, and eleven committees. The committees deal with human rights; politics; defense; agriculture; interior and public works; foreign relations and justice; culture and welfare; labor; treasury and budget; parole; and the environment. Committee assignments are made by the leadership. Each committee is led by a chair who presides over sessions, a "relator" who explains the committee recommendation to the plenary session, and a secretary who keeps track of amendments. Committee members are referred to as *vocales*. Committee sizes range from nine to thirteen members, with some members belonging to more than one committee. There are no subcommittees.

Persons who wish to initiate legislation must present their proposals to someone who has the right to introduce a bill, *iniciativa de ley*, that is, to a member of the Assembly, a judge on the Supreme Court, the president, or municipal mayors (who are allowed to present proposals relating to local taxes). Each legislative proposal is given a first reading by appointed members of the legislature; if it is deemed appropriate, it will be sent to a committee. Committees hear the bill, vote on it, and send it to a plenary session of the legislature, where it receives a second reading. If approved, it will be sent to the president, who can sign or veto the bill within eight days. The legislature must vote by a two-thirds majority to override a veto. The president has no line-item veto. The legislature also has the power to name the president and members of the Supreme Court, the president of the Central Electoral Council, and the members of the Court of Accounts (an independent auditing body for the government); these powers can impede the workings of government to a significant degree if exercised by a majority that opposes the president.

One of the stronger means the legislature has of monitoring the actions of the executive branch is the power to summon persons and papers—the power of *antejuicio*—which enables the leadership to call before the legislature any cabinet minister or even the president for open testimony. However, the party of the right, the National Republican Alliance (ARENA) is in control of both the executive and legislative branches, so it has used its majority in the chamber to prevent an antejuicio deemed to be potentially embarrassing to the party. (On occasion during the early 1990s, grilling by the legislature has brought cabinet secretaries to tears.) If the legislature and executive branches were in opposing parties, the antejuicio could be an instrument to embarrass the executive.

Perhaps the most immediate limiting factor in legislative power is the extraordinarily small staffing available for the legislators. Except for secretarial work, virtually all research must be performed by the legislators themselves, many of whom have other jobs. This forces the Assembly to rely on the language of interest groups and government ministries in preparing legislation, further diminishing the potential for autonomy. Until funding increases to permit the institution to develop an organizational capacity, the legislature's impact on politics is likely to remain minimal. The U.S. government has assisted the Assembly by finding a team of Salvadoran specialists to train legislative staff in various fields, including budgetary analysis and computer data basing. U.S. funds also helped rebuild the legislature's aging building. But in spite of these efforts, only the leaders of the legislature are given office space; the rest must share large rooms with members of their own parties.

A good deal of the internal administration of the legislature is delegated to a small staff headed by a man who has done this job since the late 1970s, when military officers dominated politics. The power he wields over individual legislators, derived from his relationship with the top leadership of the legislature under four presidents, is considerable because he controls the small administrative budget, even though he is not himself elected.

Turnover in the legislature has been steady. Of the sixty members elected in 1982, only two were still in the legislature after the 1991 elections. Recruitment and retention is made difficult because legislative salaries are low and reflect the notion that legislators work on government business for only a few weeks per year.

The Party System and the Legislature

Including the 1982 elections for the Constituent Assembly, seven rounds of elections have been held:

1982 Constituent Assembly
1984 President
1985 Legislature and municipal elections
1988 Legislature and municipal elections
1989 President
1991 Legislature and municipal elections
1994 President, legislature, and municipal elections

Table 2.1 shows party representation in the national legislature from 1982 to 1991. Of the sixteen political parties that participated in these elections, only five were active before 1982, and of these only three maintain significant electoral strength: the PDC, MNR, and PCN. Of the eleven new parties that organized during the 1980s, only five are significant: ARENA, MAC, AD, MPSC, and PSD. But because three parties (the MNR, MPSC, and PSD) have formed an electoral coalition that acts for all practical purposes as a single party, the current political system appears to have four or possibly five stable groupings, configured approximately as follows:

FMLN	CD	PDC PCN		ARENA
Extreme Left	Center-Left	Center	Center-Right	Extreme Right

Table 2.1 Party Representation in the National Legislature

Year		PDC	ARENA	PCN	CD	MAC	Other
1982	Percent	40	29	19	—	—	12
	Seats	24	19	14	—	—	3
1985	Percent	52	30	19	—	—	8
	Seats	33	13	12	—	—	2
1988	Percent	35	48	9	—	—	8
	Seats	25	32	3	—	—	—
1991	Percent	28	44	9	12	>5	>5
	Seats	26	39	9	8	1	1

Source: Compiled from data contained in various editions of *Estudios Centroamericanos,* Universidad Centroamericana, San Salvador.

Until 1989 the left did not participate in elections, creating a legislature that was polarized between the PDC and ARENA. Only during the 1985–1988 period did a single party control both the legislature and the presidency (the PDC under Duarte), a period of maximum dependency on U.S. assistance for the war effort, a situation that appears to have reduced ideological polarization. In 1989, a portion of the left participated in presidential elections, drawing only 4 percent of the vote, and then in 1991 participated in legislative elections, garnering nearly 10 percent of the seats in the legislature.

It is unclear what kind of party system will emerge now that the left is participating in politics, much less what effect there will be on the functioning of the legislature. It appears there will be at least three main groupings of parties representing a wide ideological range, but the degree of polarization that arises will depend on the pattern of discourse that develops between the left and right, as well as on the evolution of the ideology of major parties. Whether the party system moves the legislature in a centripetal or centrifugal direction, to use Sartori's terminology,[7] will depend in large part on the political culture that emerges in the next few years. If the left, center, and right establish stable groupings of parties and develop a culture of dialogue, a centrist logic may develop; if not, the system may continue to be highly polarized and centrifugal in nature.

The effect that changes occurring in the party system may have on the relative power of the legislature is unclear. Until recently politics in El Salvador has played out in two separate arenas. In one arena, democratic formality—unfairly constituted—defined the rules of political conflict. Presidents and legislatures were duly elected (usually on schedule), policies were debated, and laws were passed. Potential threats to absolute oligarchic rule in the form of politically organized groups were simply defined as falling outside the formal policy and were denied access to formal power.

In another arena, which varied in importance from time to time, political conflict played out through the rules of warfare. The left organized; eluded the armed forces' repressive apparatus as best it could; pressured for concessions with individuals, corporations, government agencies, and the like; and tried, when possible, to overthrow the government. The right, in turn, using formal and informal means, tried to minimize the threat.

Today, El Salvador is experimenting for the first time since the 1920s with a formula that would place both the left and right in the same arena, with guarantees from the international community that the rules will be equally applied. The scale of the effort to accomplish this task is mammoth because it involves major changes in the habits of key institutions such as the electoral tribunal and the armed forces, as well as major changes in attitude on the part of the left. The success of the effort so far has required the full support of the United Nations and, for the first time in many decades, direct dialogue between the representatives of the left and right. Thus, the influence that the party system may have on the functioning of the legislature is unclear because the system itself will be defined by the successes and failures of the current effort to incorporate the left.

Conclusion

In spite of efforts undertaken by the U.S. government to upgrade the organizational capacity of the legislature, the Assembly's prominence as a political actor is likely to remain secondary. There is virtually no history of legislative autonomy, nor has anyone yet emerged to champion a stronger legislature. Under these conditions, major political actors are unlikely to imagine positively a political system with an autonomous legislature having strong watchdog functions and an independent capacity to analyze, probe, and monitor. More likely, the legislature will continue to be perceived as a place where decisions made in other arenas are legitimized by majority vote. The major issue in Salvadoran politics has to do with the rules of the game in those other arenas. If the main players in Salvadoran politics can reach a working relationship about these rules, they will not need to strengthen the legislature; if they cannot, they will be unable to strengthen the legislature.

Whether the legislature will grow stronger depends on factors still in flux—the degree of polarity and organizational capacity that develops within the party system, and the ability to form a political consensus to accord the legislature a significant role in managing national conflict. This consensus has never developed in the past.

Notes

1. Maria and Freddy Leistenschneider, *Gobernantes de El Salvador* (San Salvador: Publicaciones Ministerio del Interior, 1980), p. 73.

2. Manuel Vidal, *Nociones de Historia de Centroamerica,* 9th edition (San Salvador: Ministerio de Educacion, 1982), p. 231.

3. Compiled from *Peridos Presidenciales y Constituciones Federales y Politicas de El Salvador,* compiled by Maria and Freddy Leistenschneider, Coleccion antropolgia e historia, No. 17 (San Salvador: Administracion del Partimonio Cultural, 1979).

4. Maria and Freddy Leistenschneider, *Gobernantes de El Salvador,* p. 75.

5. Ibid., p. 74. For a conservative view of Malespin's administration, see Jose Antonio Cevallos, *Recuerdos Salvadorenos,* Tomo III (San Salvador: Ministerio de Educacion, 1965).

6. For a recent analysis of the peace accords, see Joseph G. Sullivan, "How Peace Came to El Salvador," *Orbis,* Winter 1994, pp. 83–98.

7. For an analysis of polarization effects, see Giovanni Sartori, *Parties and Party System: A Framework for Analysis* (Cambridge: Cambridge University Press, 1976); and Manfred J. Holler (ed.), *The Logic of Multiparty Systems* (Dordrecht, the Netherlands: Kluwer Academic, 1987), cited in Cordova, "Procesos Electorales." Cordova argues that the Salvadoran case during the late 1980s is anomalous in that Sartori does not anticipate a system that is simultaneously bipolar, highly polarized, and centrifugal.

3

Nicaragua: The Legislature as Seedbed of Conflict

David Close

Since her election as president of Nicaragua in 1990, Violeta Chamorro has been engaged in a continuing struggle with the country's National Assembly (Asamblea Nacional) over the pace and scope of political change. This would be unremarkable were the legislature not controlled by her own party, the National Opposition Union (UNO), an alliance formed specifically for the 1990 elections. The issue dividing the legislative and executive wings of the party is how quickly and how thoroughly they should dismantle a decade's revolutionary government under the Sandinista National Liberation Front (FSLN, or the Frente). President Chamorro and her cabinet favor a moderate pace that leaves the Frente some political space and preserves parts of the revolutionary agenda, e.g., land reform. Her legislative caucus is pushing for the greatest possible "de-Sandinization" in the shortest time. Chamorro wants to minimize the chances of conflict; the UNO in the Assembly is less concerned about this.

Unquestionably, the National Assembly has a central role in contemporary Nicaraguan politics, and the way it performs that role will influence the nation's chances of consolidating a liberal democratic polity. It is, however, not clear that the Assembly's influence will be positive. Because both the issues at stake and the institutions where they will be resolved are products of the Sandinista period, this study of the legislature's contribution to building democracy in Nicaragua must start there.

Background: Sandinista Legislatures

Nicaragua has little history of representative government to build on. From 1937 to 1979, when the Somoza family ran Nicaragua like its private firm, the legislature was notable because the dictator's opponents

were guaranteed one-third, then later 40 percent, of the seats regardless of electoral outcomes. When the Sandinistas ousted the dynasty,
prospects for a functioning legislature were little better. The FSLN was
a Marxist-populist organization that had just emerged victorious from
eighteen years of guerrilla warfare. Its view of democracy emphasized
outcomes and social and economic equality, not institutions and procedures.

Although the Frente viewed governmental machinery as an instrument to build socialism better, its first attempt at constructing a representative assembly was both novel and controversial. The Council of
State (Consejo de Estado) was a curiosity among legislatures because
its members were appointed, not elected, and represented economic,
political, and social groups instead of geographic constituencies.
Though Churchill and De Gaulle mused about corporate chambers,
they paired them with conventional, popularly elected houses. A uni-
cameral, totally corporate body broke new ground.

Originally proposed by the Sandinista-aligned United People's
Movement (MPU) before Somoza fell, the Council was to bring
together all the organizations pushing for the dictator's removal.
Because opposition to Somoza was widespread, even groups such as
COSEP (Superior Council of Private Enterprise) that opposed any
socialist project were among the twenty-three organizations that would
share thirty-three seats. This hardly sat well with the FSLN; thus, when
the Somoza government reneged on its promise to hand over power
peacefully and opened the way to a Sandinista military triumph, the
radicals reconsidered their position.

The Frente complained that the Council of State was not representative. Not only had some of the original members passed out of
existence, having been ad hoc fronts, but none of the various
Sandinista mass organizations held seats. Because these groups were
key components in the revolutionary state's political plans, their exclusion was intolerable.

To remedy these shortcomings, the Sandinista-controlled governing council (the Junta, or the JGRN), the country's executive, unilat-
erally added fourteen seats, bringing the Council of State to forty-
seven members, later adding another four (see Table 3.1). Because
several original members had disappeared, the additional seats
brought more than fourteen new actors into the chamber. The result
was that the Sandinistas (the FSLN, its mass organizations, and the military) got twenty-four seats and had reliable allies with seven more.
Their opponents, mainly but not exclusively from the right, held barely a third of the places.

Table 3.1 Composition of the Council of State, 1984

Organization	Seats
FSLN	6
Sandinista Defense Committees (CDS)	9
Sandinista Youth (JS-19)	1
Nicaraguan Women's Association (AMNLAE)	1
Armed Forces (EPS)	1
Rural Workers' Union (ATC)	2
Sandinista Workers' Central (CST)	3
National Farmers' and Ranchers' Union (UNAG)	2
Nicaraguan Teachers' Association	1
Federation of Health Workers (Fetsalud)	1
Union of Journalists (UPN)	1
Independent Liberal Party (PLI)	1
Popular Social Christian Party (PPSC)	1
Nicaraguan Federation of Trade Unions (CTN)	1
Democratic Conservative Party (PCD)	1
Social Christian Party (PSC)	1
Nicaraguan Democratic Movement (MDN)	1
Nicaraguan Socialist Party (PSN)	1
Constitutionalist Liberal Movement (MLC)	1
General Federation of Labor—Independent (CGT-I)	2
Council of Trade Union Unity (CUS)	1
COSEP	6
Confederation of Professional Associations (CONAPRO)	1
Association of Clergy (ACLEN)	1
Ecumenical Axis	1
Council of Higher Education	1
Center for Union Action and Unity (CAUS)	2

This gesture did two things. First, probably as intended, it reversed the balance of forces in the original allotment[1] that had given the Frente twelve of thirty-three seats; a pro-FSLN bloc eleven; COSEP six; seven for the FAO (Broad Oppositional Front), whom the Sandinistas distrusted; and two for genuine independents. Even if only at a symbolic level, the change showed who would be the architect of the revolution. The second consequence was the withdrawal of the right from Sandinista government. However much this may have pleased the FSLN's leaders, it ensured that the Council of State would not be a central political actor. With both big business and the political right not represented—even if by their own choosing—the Council would lack credibility.

All of the Sandinistas' efforts to assure themselves of a solid majority in the Council are hard to understand in light of the legislature's very limited powers. Conventionally called a "colegislative" body, to indicate that it shared lawmaking duties with the JGRN, the legislature was plainly the junior partner. Among the powers enumerated in its General Statute[2] were: approving or amending bills submitted by the Junta; presenting its own bills to the Junta; preparing an elections act and a constitution when the JGRN asked for them; and requesting, through the JGRN, reports from ministries and government enterprises (Article 6). It could not override the Junta's veto (Article 19), it had no budget role (Article 27f), and bills from the Junta on which it did not act in ten days were deemed passed.[3]

Because of the combined legal and political limitations affecting the Council of State, it is surprising to find that the Council accomplished anything. It occasionally defeated legislation, though nothing submitted by the JGRN,[4] but this was less important than two other achievements. First, the Council proved a very useful place to do detailed studies of complex and contentious issues. This was especially evident in the debates on the 1983 Political Parties Law (in which the FSLN renounced the legal bases of one-partyism) and the 1984 Electoral Law (which established both an electoral system and the offices to be elected). Thus, a representative assembly found a niche in the Sandinista policy process. Second, and more important though less tangible, the routine operations of the Council of State opened parts of the policy process to public scrutiny and began accustoming people to the idea of a legal, civic opposition.

When the Council of State closed its doors for the last time in 1984, it marked the end of Sandinista experiments with exotic representative forums. The Council's successor, the National Assembly, is sufficiently orthodox in form and operation that the revolutionaries' conservative heir uses it effectively. But changing the legislature's

Table 3.2   Representation in the Nicaraguan National Assembly, 1985–1990

Party	Seats
FSLN	61
Democratic Conservatives (PCD)	14
Independent Liberals (PLI)	9
Popular Social Christians (PPSC)	6
Communists (PCN)	2
Socialists (PSN)	2
Popular Action Movement (MAP)	2
Total	96

name and structure did not solve its problems. In its first session (1985–1990) the National Assembly displayed the same strengths and weaknesses as did the Council of State.

Nicaragua's 1984 Electoral Law set out the groundwork for the new legislature: ninety members (*diputados*), each with an alternate (*suplente*), returned by proportional representation from the country's nine administrative districts, with a provision for seating the defeated presidential candidate of any party that won one-ninetieth (1.1 percent) of the national vote. The electoral system benefited small parties because all regional remainders were put into a national pool,[5] improving a party's chance of getting at least the 1.1 percent needed to see its presidential hopeful in the legislature. As a result, this put the maximum number of parties in the new Assembly, enhancing the Sandinistas' democratic credentials and broadening the base of representation (see Table 3.2). Although the government attempted to change the electoral system in 1988 to strengthen larger parties (and stem the proliferation of microparties that began after the signing of the Esquipulas Accords in August 1987), it was unable to do so. Thus, it is this system that was in use for the 1990 elections.

With the new look came new powers. The 1987 Constitution, elaborated in the Assembly, lets the legislature override a presidential veto with an absolute majority (Article 143), summon and question members of the executive (Article 138.4), and gives it a place in the budgetary process (Article 138.6). But the new look did not include the presence of the most vigorous anti-Sandinistas. Two of the parties in the chamber, the Conservative Democrats and the Independent Liberals, ran on rightist platforms in 1984, but neither really claimed the allegiance of the right. That went to the Nicaraguan Democratic Coordinator (Coordinadora), an umbrella organization composed of unions, parties, and COSEP. The organization's parties had not run in 1984, claiming the election was fraudulent, leaving a critical part of the political spectrum unrepresented.

The Assembly also suffered because it had little opportunity to oversee the executive. Not only were both the executive and legislative branches of Nicaragua's government solidly controlled by the FSLN, but the National Assembly had few tools that it could use independently; for example, it did not actually begin to review national budgets until 1989. Opposition deputies could raise issues in debate, but not much more.

Although these limitations slowed the development of the National Assembly as a policy actor, they did not stop it altogether. The trajectory set in the Council of State continued. This translated, first, into doing a great deal of detail work, mainly through an active and extensive committee system. It also meant that the media continued paying attention to the legislature: the country's three dailies, the TV network, and the major radio stations all had reporters covering the legislative beat. So Nicaraguans were informed, though far from impartially, about how some national policies were made and what their elected representatives were doing. Nicaraguans also saw that at least some forms of political opposition were acceptable and that controversy about public issues sometimes spawned positive outcomes.

M. Mezey proposes a policy classification of legislatures (see Table 3.3) that helps put the two Sandinista-era legislatures into perspective.[6] Whereas the Council of State began as something close to a minimal legislature that was a rubber stamp, nine years later the National Assembly was much more a marginal legislature, with a restricted policymaking function. Beginning with the Political Parties Law of 1983, continuing through the constitution-making process of 1985–1986, and concluding with the elaboration of significant legislation on local government in 1988, Nicaragua's representative institutions evolved into useful, if limited, "policy refineries."[7] This developmental path ended after the FSLN was swept from office in the 1990 elections. Since then, the National Assembly has become more confrontational toward the executive, seeking an independent policy role.

Table 3.3   A Policy Impact Classification of Legislatures

Class (Characteristics)	Example
Active (Autonomous and active policymaker)	U.S. Congress
Reactive (Reacts to and influences policy)	Canadian Parliament
Marginal (Minor adjunct to executive policymaking)	Nicaraguan National Assembly
Minimal (Executive-dominated rubber stamp)	Somoza Congress/ Supreme Soviet

Source: Adapted from Hague, et al., *Comparative Government and Politics* (London: Macmillan, 1992), p. 298.

The Seeds of Executive-Legislative Conflict

Nicaraguans discarded revolutionary democracy and the politics of socialist transformation when they voted the Sandinistas out of office in February 1990 and brought in the UNO. That they wanted the FSLN out was clear from the results: 54.1 percent of the votes went to the UNO, 40 percent to the Sandinistas, and the rest to the also-rans. The UNO would control both the presidency and the National Assembly (see Table 3.4), but how it would exercise that control was not clear.

Table 3.4 Nicaraguan National Assembly, 1990

Party/Faction	Seats
UNO	51
FSLN	39
Yatama[a]	1[b]
Revolutionary Unity Movement	1[b]

Notes: a. The regional party from the Northern Atlantic Autonomous Region.
b. Votes with UNO.

One line of thought—sustained by President Chamorro, her cabinet and advisors, and the FSLN—says that the election was about peace and reconstruction. Throughout the Sandinista years the Nicaraguan state fought a difficult and costly war against U.S.-backed counterrevolutionary insurgents. Washington gave no sign of letting up if the Sandinistas were reelected, so Nicaraguans voted rationally to return an administration that could get along with the White House and end the destruction. A postelection survey done by the Sandinista-linked Institute for Nicaraguan Studies supports this interpretation;[8] fully two-thirds of declared UNO voters identified promises to end the military draft and secure peace as the most attractive parts of the winners' platform.

Not everyone holds this view. The UNO began as an electoral alliance, bringing together most of those who opposed the Frente for any reason. Thus, it harbored Socialists, Communists, Liberals, Conservatives, Christian Democrats, and Central American integrationists. Because the party issued a program[9] that included (1) the return of properties expropriated by the revolutionary government (V.5) and (2) the restructuring of security forces to remove all traces of Sandinista influence (IV.4–5), those who wanted to enact it rapidly could point to their landslide victory as a mandate. The fact that the campaign was built around a general theme of change (the UNO slogan was "*Que se vayan*"—"Out with them") only strengthened the convictions of this group.

Though there may be circumstances that would let these views be reconciled constructively, they did not exist in Nicaragua in 1990. Those who wanted the letter of the platform enacted immediately formed the bulk of UNO members and the majority in the National Assembly. Unistas who believed in gradualism were concentrated in the executive. The Sandinistas added their own fuel to the fire: first, by promising to "govern from below," i.e., to mobilize a powerful extraparliamentary opposition; second, by being unable to keep in line the unions and other groups affiliated with them; third, by passing controversial legislation in a lame-duck session of the National Assembly after the 1990 electoral loss; finally, by using their thirty-nine seats in the house to back some of President Chamorro's policies, leading to charges of "cogovernment" or Sandinista domination of the executive.

All of these factors have combined to set the National Assembly, its UNO majority more precisely, against the president and her cabinet. The conflict has been in the making since 1979 when the Sandinistas rose to power, but it blossomed in the two months between the election and Chamorro's inauguration.

Chamorro's first task was to prepare for the transfer of power. She designated a team led by her son-in-law, and later minister of the presidency and de facto prime minister, Antonio Lacayo. The FSLN responded with one headed by General Humberto Ortega, the minister of defense and brother of President Daniel Ortega. On March 27, 1990, the two teams released the text of the Protocol for the Transfer of the Executive Power of the Republic of Nicaragua, the transition accords,[10] which included these provisions:

1. The armed forces would be professional and apolitical, and members on active service could not hold leadership positions in any party.
2. People who had received urban or rural property from the Sandinista state before the elections should be given secure title, and those who lost property should be compensated.
3. Vindictiveness, reprisals, and revenge have no place in the transition. Thus, existing associations, unions, and community organizations will continue to exist and enjoy normal, constitutional protections. In the same spirit, monuments commemorating Sandinista heroes are to be respected.
4. Government employment would be based on efficiency, honesty, and years of service, not partisan affiliation.

In return for not purging Sandinistas from government or proscribing Sandinista unions, and for accepting that properties distributed over a decade could not be returned to the previous owners without creating enormous problems, Chamorro got a go-ahead to reduce the size of the military. Doña Violeta, as she is universally known in the country, carried this policy a step further when she announced at her inauguration that General Ortega would continue to command the Nicaraguan army. Seen in one light, the incoming administration put some of its platform on hold to get peace and stability; but from the viewpoint of UNO's hardliners, it was a sellout.

Even this might have been borne were it not for the Sandinistas' "piñata." This was the name given to acts passed by the lame-duck Sandinista National Assembly to secure the property rights mentioned in the transition accords. What earned them this label (for which the best translation here is "grab bag") was whose property was being protected. It was not so much that the legislation protected a peasant on a few acres of scrubland or woman and her kids in a little house in Managua; these were expected. But when Daniel Ortega got title to one of Managua's fanciest mansions and the rest of the Sandinista hierarchy did nearly as well, battle lines were drawn.

The Institutional and Partisan Environment

Though the National Assembly works with essentially the same rules under the UNO as under the Sandinistas, a combination of an executive committed to building constitutional government and a majority that escapes the executive's discipline has produced a very strong and active legislature. This happened because the institutional framework itself leaves the legislature some resources, physical and legal, with which to combat the executive.

Since 1980, Nicaragua's legislatures have been located in the old central bank building, not in the quarters once occupied by Somoza's Congress.[11] The building houses the floor of the Assembly in a large rotunda, as well as offices for the Assembly's executive committee (known as the JD) and administrative staff. Deputies do not have individual offices, but parties or parliamentary factions get space in the former Banco de América building just across the street. Other facilities for members are equally sparse; for example, there are no committee rooms, so meetings are held in the open on the building's mezzanine. There is, however, a printed record of debates (though costs limit its distribution), and members get coffee and cookies served to them in their seats.

Deputies are arranged on either side of an aisle—the majority sit

to the speaker's left, speak while seated, and have not yet developed
the formal language associated with the Canadian Parliament or the
U.S. Congress. Debates are lively, strongly partisan, but not devoid of
substance. Proceedings are formally controlled by the JD, made up of
a president or speaker, two vice-presidents, and three secretaries, all of
whom are deputies elected by their peers. Having a six-person executive makes ticket balancing among parties and factions necessary, and
selecting the JD can be a contentious issue. A solid press corps has
developed, and reporting on the legislature is quite good in both *La
Prensa* (pro-UNO but anti-Chamorro, even though it is her family's
paper) and *Barricada* (pro-Sandinista, formerly the Frente's official
paper).

Nicaragua's National Assembly enjoys three constitutionally
assigned powers that make it a potentially formidable force: veto override, constitutional amendment, and constitutional interpretation.
Article 143 of the Nicaraguan Constitution allows the National
Assembly to override a presidential veto by an absolute majority of all
members. This is a relatively easy override provision, but the Assembly
has not been able to muster the necessary votes for any critical legislation. The Assembly is also the sole source of constitutional amendments, which in the past it could approve only with a 60 percent majority (Article 194) in *two* legislatures (Article 192).[12] This has been
particularly important to the UNO majority, who wish to make significant changes to the document but have fallen just short of the
required numbers.

Finally, Article 138.2 empowers the National Assembly to render
an official and binding interpretation of the law. This provision is the
functional equivalent of judicial review in Canada or the United States
and presumably lets the legislature determine the meaning of the
Constitution as well as of ordinary laws. In 1991, for example, a number of UNO deputies sought an official interpretation of the president's veto power, but the session ended before the issue was considered by the whole house. Although this seems a useful way to amend
the Constitution by stealth, it has never been used.

None of these powers would mean much if the bulk of the UNO
caucus did not oppose the president who led them to power. The legislative and executive wings of the party have different agendas, partly
because the two have different backgrounds. C. Vilas points out
that the executive is staffed by business leaders and professionals,
many related to Chamorro, who did not suffer directly under the
revolutionary government.[13] The legislative faction, however, is home
to those who were hardest hit by nationalizations. As a senior member
of the executive branch put it in an interview,[14] the UNO caucus is

made up of people who lost their property or those people's lawyers.

Having felt the heavier hand of Sandinista rule, the UNO's legislative caucus wants to move the country as far from that model of government as fast as it can. Chamorro's advisors, on the other hand, fear that social and political instability will result if the change from the old regime to the new is too abrupt. Conflicts about the pace of change between the two factions of the 1990 electoral alliance have produced dramatic executive-legislative clashes over the defense budget and the disposition of property expropriated by the Sandinista government.

Facing a divided governing party has put the FSLN in a curious position. Though it opposes the president's laissez-faire economic policies, it finds the proposals of the UNO legislative caucus even harder to accept. Moreover, the executive wants stability, so it is willing to deal with the Sandinistas, unlike the "impossibilists" in the Assembly who will never compromise with the former governors. This has led to the Frente supporting a number of administration proposals, even becoming the key to a shaky pro-Chamorro alliance in the house. As a result, UNO's anti-Chamorro wing has charged that the president has brought the revolutionaries into her administration, creating a Chamorro-Sandinista cogovernment that they are determined to destroy.

Three Conflicts

Doña Violeta has not had an easy presidential term. Most new chief executives have a honeymoon with voters, the press, and the opposition that lasts for several months. Hers ended the day she took office because she retained Sandinista general Humberto Ortega as Nicaragua's top soldier. A decision made to keep the army calm and to quiet Sandinista fears about reprisals unleashed a storm of criticism from conservative politicians and former contra soldiers who saw Ortega as their number one enemy. Before long, the criticism turned into fierce parliamentary opposition from the UNO benches to Chamorro's defense budget and created the administration's first crisis with the legislature.

The Defense Budget

That her colleagues wanted to be rid of Sandinista influence in Nicaragua's military should not have surprised the president. Since the early days of the revolutionary government, the right, led by COSEP, had made the security forces a prime target. They were particularly concerned that all the security forces carried the label *Sandinista* (e.g., the Sandinista Popular Army [EPS] and the Sandinista Police [PS]), not *Nicaraguan;* and they interpreted this to mean that the armed services responded to a party instead of the nation. When the EPS received constitutional status in 1987 (Article 95), meaning that a constitutional amendment was required to change the organization's name, the anti-Sandinistas' worst fears were confirmed.

The contras, of course, wanted no part of their old nemesis. Oscar Sobalvarro, Comandante Reuben, said the insurgents' disarmament was conditional on the "disappearance" of the EPS.[15] Another contra commander, Israel Galeano, Comandante Franklin, suggested that the one-time rebels act as the president's guard until the EPS was disbanded: "We are going to help Doña Violeta with our guns and our hands inside the national territory. We will lay down our arms only when there is total demobilization."[16]

President Chamorro likely accepted retaining Humberto Ortega as the price to pay for the high command's help in downsizing the military. Ten years of counterinsurgency warfare left Nicaragua with an estimated 80,000 regular troops and a defense bill that may have been as high as 60 percent of the budget in 1987–1988.[17] Any economic future the country had was dependent on putting national security money to more productive uses. Thus, the president announced, and the general agreed, that troop strength would be halved by the end of 1990. This would save money, would leave the army strong enough to maintain internal control, and would not put too many demobilized soldiers out on the streets.

It was a fine plan that did not translate well into practice. The UNO voted unanimously to reduce the proposed defense budget from $78 million (already down from $166 million the year before) to $58 million. Chamorro immediately vetoed the Assembly's bill, saying that the reduction of the military had to be gradual and noting that in less than a year she had shrunk the armed forces from 80,000 to 28,400 members.[18] The next week, after intense lobbying by the executive[19] and a promise to cut about $8 million from the original estimate, the legislature sustained Chamorro's veto, 69-21. Had the veto been overturned, the president indicated that it would have meant slashing another 10,000 troops from the military.

Further cuts, though, were what the UNO caucus still wanted, and they came back the next year to get them. The 1992 budget, debated in late 1991, brought another showdown between Doña Violeta and what should have been her legislative majority. In November, the president sent the National Assembly a budget asking for about $42 million for defense, 60 percent of the previous year's allotment. Because the size of the forces had dropped from 28,000 to 21,000, this should have been a workable proposal.

However, the UNO deputies wanted more drastic reductions. They complained that the military had not intervened the week before when Sandinista sympathizers, outraged after a bomb damaged the tomb of FSLN founder Carlos Fonseca, attacked Managua's city hall and an anti-Sandinista radio station. Vice-president Virgilio Godoy, one of the mainstays of the anti-Chamorro wing of the UNO, "charged that the violence demonstrated the incapacity of the government to control the Sandinistas, saying that the armed forces did not heed Chamorro's call to control the violence."[20] As a result, the UNO proposed cutting $4.3 million from the funds earmarked for the military.

This time, though, the administration's proposal passed, 47-45, thanks to the votes of all thirty-nine Sandinistas and eight Unistas, representing six parties. The handful of UNO deputies who supported the president later emerged as a pivotal political force, the Center Group. However, it was less the defense budget than the way National Assembly president Alfredo César managed the delicate property question that spawned the new legislative group.

Returning Expropriated Property

When they took power in 1979 the Sandinistas issued Decree 3, seizing the properties of the Somozas and their associates. Some of this property became state farms or factories; other holdings went to cooperatives or, especially in the case of housing, organizations and individuals. In later years, the state expropriated the holdings of those who chose to leave Nicaragua and abandon their properties (Decree 760, the "absentee law"); these, too, were redistributed. The day after the UNO's massive electoral sweep, the "confiscados" began to dream of reclaiming what the revolution had taken.

Electoral defeat also set the Sandinistas into motion. Much of the redistributed property had not been properly titled. To rectify this, a lame-duck session of the Sandinista-dominated National Assembly passed the laws that were soon labeled the "piñata." Laws 85 and 86 gave title to the residents of state-owned houses and lots, respectively; Law 88 converted all agrarian reform use titles into full ownership titles. About 80,000 families held agrarian reform titles to roughly four million acres; there were some 11,000 beneficiaries of Law 85 and 100,000 of Law 86.[21] One estimate put the value of the properties affected at upwards of $500 million.[22]

President Chamorro recognized the centrality of the issue and issued Decrees 10-90 and 11-90 in May 1990 to expedite the return of some properties, not including those expropriated from the Somozas, to their original owners. In October 1990, the president agreed to respect property distributed before February 25, 1990, and to compensate owners whose properties were unjustly expropriated.[23] But these efforts did not satisfy those who wanted their lands and houses restored to them.

On June 18, 1991, UNO legislators introduced a bill to repeal Laws 85 and 86. This prompted the Sandinista bench to walk out. That evening, Sandinista sympathizers, many of them armed, occupied six city halls, including Managua's, and three radio stations. Former president Daniel Ortega said that "this violence is the logical consequence of thousands of Nicaraguans who fear losing their land and homes."[24]

Leading the charge against the piñata was the speaker of the National Assembly, Alfredo César, once a staunch "Violetero" (Chamorro supporter). Managua's pundits interpreted this as a ploy by César to gain conservative support for an eventual run at the presidency. Even if that was not his aim, piloting the bill to its passage in August 1991 catapulted César into national prominence. By choosing to use the legislature as his springboard, César indicated that at least he thought the National Assembly had the stature to produce great leaders.

Doña Violeta and her advisors believed the act (Law 133) was too confrontational and likely to produce even further unrest. It came, then, as no surprise that the president vetoed the "Ley César" (César Law) on September 11, 1991. Because all fifty-two UNO members present had supported Law 133 and all thirty-nine Sandinistas had opposed it, the executive's problem was to find eight deputies to join the FSLN in sustaining the veto. Although the president had had little trouble making her veto stick concerning the 1990 budget, a year's hardships had since worn away some of her luster.

When the veto came to a vote in December, eight UNO members joined with the Frente to give the administration a 47-45 win. These are the same votes that stayed with the president on the budget. Why did these deputies bolt the caucus and form a "center bloc"? A Sandinista deputy offered an intriguing explanation:[25] the deputies in question were not heavyweights in the UNO. Thus, when Doña Violeta reminded them that they had ridden her coattails into Managua and so owed her something, they listened. Moreover, the president suggested that people who supported her could find favors coming their way: somebody has to recommend who should be a judge or where a new bridge should go. Finally, Alfredo César's unwillingness to persuade these waverers to stay with him (he reportedly first ignored their concerns, then threatened them) made them easy targets for Chamorro's warm manner.

But even if César lost the battle over the veto, he had not lost the war. He had seriously challenged the president's program by mobilizing the legislature's conservative majority. In doing so he showed that the National Assembly had attained enough strength to make it a formidable resource in the hands of an able and ambitious politician. In September 1992 he would have his most memorable hour, using the National Assembly to defy Nicaragua's constitutional order.

César's Legislative Coup

The most serious executive-legislative clash began in mid-1992. Two members of the JD resigned their posts for personal reasons, but César delayed filling them because it seemed that a Sandinista and a centrist would be elected.[26] His dilatory tactics spurred a walkout by the FSLN and the pro-Chamorro Unistas—forty-seven deputies in all, over half the members. This left the National Assembly without a quorum, set at an absolute majority (forty-seven in this case) by the Constitution (Article 141). The stalemate broke after a tidal wave smashed Nicaragua's Pacific coast on September 1, 1993; the FSLN–center bloc deputies returned for a sitting, still found the situation unattractive, and withdrew again. But Alfredo César had seen enough, and he convened a rump parliament built around the remaining forty-five UNO deputies.

César's action brought an immediate court challenge from the FSLN-center alliance. A Managua appeals court upheld the challenge but without effect. Luis Sánchez, the Assembly's vice-president, acting in César's absence, ignored the ruling. He argued that the court had no right to make the legislature enforce its own rules and that, in any case, the court was an institution inferior to the legislature.[27] Nevertheless, Sánchez appealed the decision.

While the courts were sorting out the appeals, César convened the Assembly, calling alternates to replace the boycotting UNO center deputies. With both a quorum and an assured majority, César began introducing and passing legislation, including a property bill modeled on the one President Chamorro had vetoed the year before. On September 29, the National Assembly ratified Decree 534, which gave the JD power to name substitutes (even if not the duly elected alternate) for absent deputies. In light of this action, the next day President Chamorro declared that all National Assembly proceedings would be illegal until its leaders complied with the earlier appeals court ruling.[28]

This bizarre episode began winding toward an end in November, when the Supreme Court ruled that all actions of the National Assembly since September 2, 1992, were null and void for want of a legal quorum. A month later, President Chamorro dismissed the JD, an act that Luis Sánchez compared to Peruvian president Fujimori's dismissal of his congress earlier in the year.[29] Eventually, on January 9, 1993, the legislature reconvened, with a legal quorum, and elected a new executive drawn from Chamorro supporters (known as Chamorristas) and Sandinistas. The legislature continued to meet through 1993, with UNO deputies showing up so that they could qualify for their paychecks, but not participating in proceedings.

That the speaker of a legislature would countenance such a flagrant violation of the rules as operating without a proper quorum suggests two things. First, the anti-Chamorro UNO legislators were so frustrated by their inability to enact their program that they were willing to provoke a constitutional crisis. Second, it also shows their inexperience with and perhaps disdain for the slow and cumbersome machinery of constitutional government. A legislative leader in the United States, for example, might well have been content to let the chief executive compile a record to run against in the next election.

One part of the outcome of this political soap opera that must please César's wing of the UNO[30] was that the Sandinistas emerged unmistakably linked to the president: cogovernment, the Chamorrista-Sandinista coalition, so often alleged, became a reality. This put the FSLN on the spot. The most obvious risk is being linked to Chamorro's economic policies; these policies have produced 60 percent unemployment and constantly worsening living standards, particularly for the poor, the Frente's natural constituency. But even if Doña Violeta's policies turn the country around, there is no guarantee that the Sandinistas would get any credit; people could simply praise the president for having toughed one out. This is why some Sandinistas began urging the Frente to withdraw its support of Chamorro and adopt a more combative and progressive stance.[31]

Transition and Consolidation:
Is Nicaragua Becoming a Representative Democracy?

To be effective parts of liberal democratic government, legislatures must do several things. First, they have to make sure the executive is held publicly accountable for its actions. They must also include all significant sectors of opinion and be able to accommodate new forces as they emerge. A third requirement is that legislative service be a use-

ful career path for aspiring leaders, not a dead end on the back benches. Finally, legislatures must be arenas of conflict resolution, at least to
the extent of allowing proponents of contending views to seek common ground.

Not all legislatures do all of these things all of the time. A weak
opposition can let the executive escape its control, an election may
leave one segment of opinion without seats, and not all issues admit
compromise. But these are temporary exceptions in functioning liberal democracies. Judged by these standards, Nicaragua's National
Assembly produces a mixed report card, so its role in consolidating a
democratic future for the country remains uncertain.

On the plus side, the National Assembly does an effective job of
criticizing the administration. With a majority, or close to it, of the
deputies opposed to the president's policies, and with the Chamorro
administration willing to let the Assembly use its powers to harass, this
is normal. The balance of forces in the legislature—pro-administra-
tion and anti-administration from both left and right—also means that
most of Nicaragua's spectrum of public opinion is represented there,
except when one or another of the parties is boycotting. Combined,
these factors explain why resourceful legislators can build national
reputations. The ascent of the right's César is being paralleled from
the left by Sandinista house leader and former Nicaraguan vice-president Sergio Ramírez.

It is as a forum for moderating conflict that the National Assembly
falls woefully short. Contemporary Nicaraguan politics does not really
allow much room for consensus. In an economically devastated country, where crime is reaching new heights and with enough armed
groups having enough different agendas to make a long and bloody
civil war an all too real possibility, a faithful reproduction of the
national political tableau might never lead to compromise. But the
control of the National Assembly by strongly confrontational forces
aggravates this difficult situation.

On balance, Nicaragua's National Assembly was, by mid-1993,
doing less to consolidate democracy in the country than to undermine
it. Whether this was the legislators' intent is immaterial, as is the fact
that there were many other forces tending in that same direction. The
Assembly has become a strong, independent political actor, and it has
used its strength, perfectly legitimately, to confront the executive and
produce an air of instability. It is unlikely that the center-left coalition
between the Sandinistas and the presidentialist wing of the UNO, even
if it endures, can do much to relieve the tension. Indeed, this alliance
may cause the more intransigent Unistas to take their struggle outside
the legislature and even outside the Constitution. A successful job of

legislature building does not, then, guarantee a successful consolidation of representative democracy.

Conclusion

Nicaragua's experience with representative institutions since 1979 offers several lessons to students and practitioners of democratization. First, the Sandinista-era legislatures showed that representative institutions can contribute to the formation of what might be called a protoconstitutional regime, even when they have little lawmaking power. The things that the Council of State and National Assembly did—ventilating opinion, openly criticizing government, and letting the public follow the process of policymaking—are critical functions of competitive political systems that legislatures perform especially well.

A second message is that a weak legislature can become a more effective one. This took two steps in Nicaragua, where the radical institutional reform creating the National Assembly opened the road for slower, evolutionary transformation. The cumulative effect produced the conditions under which a new government and a new party could invigorate the chamber and make it a key political player without a major overhaul.

Third, the experience of the Sandinista legislatures demonstrates what happens to assemblies that exclude some of the country's significant political actors. At best, doing so reduces the legislature's profile; at worst, it makes the legislature a sideshow to the real process of governing. In either case, an unrepresentative legislature can do little to build democracy or even bring conflict within the limits of a nation's constitution.

Further, recent Nicaraguan history gives some hints about the utility of viewing transitional politics through the legislative window. Obviously, most extraparliamentary conflict is omitted, though debates and resolutions regularly touch on this. But because focusing on the National Assembly reveals the questions that make up Nicaragua's grand politics, as well as the players who take various sides on these questions, it leaves a strong and accurate impression of the country's political health. Where this is not the result, the legislature may be incapable of bearing the burdens that democratic government imposes on representative assemblies.

Finally, the first three years of the Chamorro administration remind us that, though solid democracies have strong representative institutions, a powerful legislature can work against democratic consolidation in the short run. Even accepting the position of the majority of the UNO caucus that the Chamorro administration's policies retard democracy, it is difficult to see how the caucus's confrontational, all-or-nothing politics can produce more positive results. Extremism in the defense of liberty may not be a vice, but if it produces chaos, suffering, and civil war it is plainly not a virtue.

Constitutional government has always been based on toleration, whether it was Anglicans abiding Puritans in eighteenth-century England or the middle classes accepting organized labor in twentieth-century welfare states. Where toleration is absent, open conflict is not far off and democracy often imperiled. The legislature's contribution toward consolidating democracy in a transitional setting depends as much on the aims of those who control that institution as on the assembly's own powers, rules, and relations with other political forces. In the hands of intemperate leaders, the legislature can as easily produce a crisis that ends democracy as push forward democracy's cause.

Postscript

In December 1993 an intriguing new bloc formed in Nicaragua's National Assembly to support a major constitutional reform program. Coming on the heels of several months of violence that featured reciprocal hostage takings by ex-contra troops and former Sandinista soldiers and a bloody transit strike, the legislative coalition had the makings of a pact to secure stability. One sign of this was the bloc's make-up: the FSLN, the Christian Democrats—themselves an amalgam of the left and right wings of Nicaraguan Christian Democracy—the Center Group of solid Chamorro supporters, the similarly centrist Reconciliation and Unity Bloc, and the right-leaning Popular Conservative Alliance of long-time anti-Sandinista leader Miriam Arguello. A part of Nicaragua's right joined the center and left of the political spectrum to support not just a piece of legislation, but an all new constitutional design. One could think about a new governing consensus that would lead Nicaragua out of chaos.

A look at the content of the proposed amendments, however, suggests that the National Assembly had not yet become the savior of constitutional government in Nicaragua, and explains why the proposals set loose a year of furious political debate. The key change was to the amending process itself. Where previously the legislature had to produce a 60 percent majority vote two years running to amend the

Constitution, the Assembly approved an amendment that would require it to get that robust majority only once. The possibilities for turning the Constitution into a political football are patent.

Regarding substantive changes, the broad, pro-amendment bloc concentrated on weakening the executive, thus shifting more constitutional authority to itself. In particular, it focused on the question of presidential succession, introducing a consanguinity prohibition that would keep Chamorro's son-in-law from succeeding her, and limiting the president to one term with no reelection possible. As these limitations would also apply to both Sandinista ex-president Daniel Ortega and his brother, General Humberto Ortega, both left and right were placated. From this angle, however, the amendment package looks less like far-sighted leadership and more like short-term settling of accounts, log-rolling, and aggrandizement of power. The president, to no one's surprise, opposed the amendments, setting the stage for gridlock through most of 1994.

Whatever becomes of the 1993 amendment package, the jury should remain out on the Assembly's contribution to democratic consolidation for a while longer. Though heightened interparty cooperation is encouraging, these alliances have yet to stand the test of time. Should they break apart, a return to the bitter legislative conflicts of the early 1990s becomes a too real possibility. Even if they hold together, they may only heighten conflict with the executive and plunge Nicaragua into an extended bout of political stasis. Unfortunately, a strong, effective legislature cannot, by itself, guarantee democracy.

Notes

Research for this chapter was supported by a grant from the Social Sciences and Humanities Research Council of Canada.

1. There is disagreement over whether the original thirty-three seats were actually assigned. See G. Black, *The Triumph of the People* (London: Zed, 1981), p. 245; and S. Christian, *Revolution in the Family* (New York: Vintage, 1986), p. 172.

2. *Estatuto General del Consejo de Estado* (Managua: Consejo de Estado, 1979).

3. See Article 14 of the Estatuto Fundemental de la Republica de Nicaragua (Managua: Imprenta Nacional, 1979).

4. See J. Booth, *Nicaragua: The End and the Beginning* (Boulder: Westview Press, 1985), p. 39; and D. Close, *Nicaragua* (London: Pinter, 1988), p. 123.

5. To win a seat in any region a party had to meet a quota. Parties that did not win a seat had the votes they received put into a nationwide pool where the threshold of success was lower. Members of the Consejo Supremo Electoral interviewed after the 1984 election indicated that the electoral sys-

tem worked as they had expected—all competing parties got at least one seat in the National Assembly.

6. M. Mezey, *Comparative Legislatures* (Durham, North Carolina: Duke University Press, 1979).

7. *Policy refinery* is a term often used to describe the Canadian Parliament. It suggests that even though a legislature does not initiate many laws, it can have a policy role to the extent that it publicizes issues and gets piecemeal changes of detail accepted.

8. *Encuesta Pos-electoral* (Managua: Instituto de Estudios Nicaraguenses, 1990).

9. *Program de Gobierno* (Managua: Unión Nacional Oposidora, 1989).

10. Committee of Freely Elected Heads of Government, *Report on the 1990 Nicaraguan Election* (Atlanta: The Carter Center, 1990), pp. 113–114.

11. Material describing the setup and operation of the National Assembly comes from personal observation of many full sessions and committee hearings since 1983, when the Council of State was still Nicaragua's legislature.

12. This was amended in December 1993. The Nicaraguan Constitution can now be amended by a 60 percent majority in *one* assembly.

13. C. Vilas, "Family Affairs: Class, Lineage and Politics in Contemporary Nicaragua," *Journal of Latin American Studies,* Vol. 24, No. 2 (1992), pp. 309–341.

14. Interview with Tomás Delaney, Director de Asuntos Legales, Presidencia de la República de Nicaragua, Managua, Nicaragua, September 25, 1991.

15. *Barricada,* Managua, Nicaragua, March 6, 1990.

16. *New York Times,* March 6, 1990.

17. *Central America Report,* Guatemala City, Guatemala, December 8, 1989, p. 386; hereafter cited as *CAR.*

18. *Los Angeles Times,* December 16, 1990.

19. There were rumors circulating around the National Assembly that the cabinet lobbied with foreign aid money, hence buying votes.

20. *CAR,* November 22, 1991, p. 345.

21. *Envio,* Managua, Nicaragua, January–March 1993, pp. 39–40.

22. *Mesoamerica,* San José, Costa Rica, August 1991, p. 7.

23. This position came out of the first Concertación, a government, opposition, labor, and management meeting to set guidelines for policy. These were begun under the Sandinistas and are still used by the Chamorro administration. They have never achieved striking success, often because the political right has either boycotted them or set strict limits on their participation. They serve as supplemental representative forums that include nonparty political actors.

24. *Mesoamerica,* July 1991, p. 1.

25. Interview with Rogelio Ramirez, FSLN legislator, Managua, Nicaragua, October 1, 1991.

26. G. Fernandez, "The Origins of Illegality," *Barricada Internacional,* October 1992, p. 10.

27. Ibid., p. 11.

28. *CAR,* October 16, 1992, pp. 305–306.

29. *Mesoamerica,* January 1993, p. 1.

30. The anti-Chamorro wing of UNO is increasingly called UNO-APO (UNO–Patriotic Opposition Alliance). This is not an official name.

31. *Barricada Internacional,* July 1993, pp. 22–23.

4

Argentina's New Democracy: Presidential Power and Legislative Limits

Gary W. Wynia

Many Latin Americans spent the 1980s and early 1990s trying to govern democratically. Some countries tried harder than others and did much better, yet seldom were so many attempting this task simultaneously. In 1983 and 1989 the Argentines held two consecutive presidential elections for the first time in sixty years, and the Brazilians did the same for the first time in thirty years. Even in Nicaragua the once powerful and popular Sandinistas yielded to opponents who defeated them in free national elections.

These innovations defy conventional wisdom about Latin American politics. It has long been assumed that the region's political culture lacked beliefs that were essential to operating democratically. The Hispanic, authoritarian tradition; rigid social structures; and elites' reliance on crude corporatist modes to retain government control over citizens have been blamed perennially for past failures to sustain liberal democracy.[1]

Persistent and extensive underdevelopment combined with high concentrations of wealth have also long been faulted for democracy's fragility. With the exception of a few nations, most Latin Americans were said to lack sufficient economic development and social mobility to integrate all social classes into a community that can sustain honest, competitive politics. Or so it was long argued. Yet, now more than ever such conventional wisdom is challenged by events throughout the region.[2]

National elections have started the process by making it possible for leaders to institutionalize new rules, but this is only the beginning, as everyone has discovered. In particular, it is always difficult to build a proficient legislative process that can function in political systems that have relied on a strong executive to rule in a traditionally author-

itarian manner. That is why today the issue is less one of how to design
and launch a democracy than it is about how to consolidate and sustain its component parts.

How "Unnatural" Is Democracy in Argentina?

Democracy allows control over rulers by the ruled using stated procedures (e.g., free elections, free speech, right to organize and oppose).
This kind of politics requires what Robert Dahl calls a mix of "participation" and "contestation." Citizens must participate freely and
responsibly, and they must be allowed to organize and compete in the
electoral and policy processes. Each of these activities in turn relies on
fundamental rules to regulate such conduct (e.g., liberties guaranteed
by law, executive and legislative procedures and limits, etc.).
Democracy also releases egocentric interests that often foster conflicts
among individuals and groups. Few of these disputes are ever resolved
definitively by democratic procedures; rather, they are temporarily suspended by agreement according to formal rules. Even fundamental
constitutional provisions are not immutable; they, too, can be changed
according to the rules that govern the reform process.[3]

Democracy does not ensure citizen welfare; rather, it assumes that
reasonable welfare will be achieved by intelligent, beneficent, rational
leadership, even though that which is rational is seldom obvious to
everyone. Democracy must rely on some combination of elections to
select representatives who can enact, implement, and adjudicate policies that affect welfare.[4]

This is well known, but understanding how democracy works does
not make it any easier to sustain it in societies where traditional informal rules, not formal ones, have governed political conflict resolution
in undemocratic ways. To ask people to forsake the ways they have
resolved disputes, often in defiance of constitutional constraints and
occasionally violently, is to demand a major switch in fundamental
behaviors. Yet today that is exactly what some Argentines are asking
their fellow citizens to do. It is neither natural nor facile for several
reasons.

To begin with, Argentines did not prepare themselves very well for
what they are now attempting. They wrote a liberal democratic constitution in 1853 and expanded the male electorate wide enough to allow
middle-class voting in 1916, when the conservative incumbents were
defeated in the first of three consecutive presidential elections. But
then democracy ended. A military coup in 1930 halted competitive

politics, and in 1945 the Peronist monopoly was created. After Juan Peron was sent into exile in 1955, neither the armed forces nor civilian political parties could govern the deeply divided nation for very long. Not until 1983, after the armed forces' disastrous war with Britain in the Malvinas Islands, did the officers retreat in disgrace and permit open competitive elections. It was the start of a reform effort that is only a decade old.[5]

Argentines had also developed ways to run civilian governments that hindered democratization. They became accustomed to a very personalistic, hyperpresidential regime. The public, regardless of social class, expected the nation to be directed and protected by a single person. The upper class turned to several different persons before 1916; the reformist, middle-class Radicals relied on Hipolito Yrigoyen until he was deposed by the armed forces in 1930; and the working class became devoted to Juan and Evita Peron after 1945. Consequently, presidents often interpreted their election not as an opportunity to represent everyone but as an opportunity to preside over them. This habit was augmented by frequent economic crises during the postwar era that caused everyone to look for "solutions" imposed by the nation's first and foremost rule maker.

Not surprisingly, virtually no Argentine president in this century took constitutional checks and balances among the three branches of government very seriously. They could not ignore Congress entirely when it existed, but they used it primarily to ratify their own policies. Presidents also became notorious for issuing *decretos* (decrees) that launched policies that Congress resisted, claiming that their actions were legal under emergency provisions in the Constitution.

Political parties have distorted and abused democratic politics as well. Before 1983 civilian political parties participated in what Argentines have termed the *juego corrupto* (corrupt game). By this they meant that party leaders not only competed with one another when the opportunity for elections arose, but at one time or another each of them also did what they could to promote military coups to evict an opponent from office. An "all or nothing" mentality, not an art of sensible compromise, prevailed. Conservatives before World War II and Peronists afterward ignored their rivals and fed themselves with convictions that they were the only ones who deserved to govern the nation.

After 1955 civilian as well as military leaders only perpetuated this by trying repeatedly to demolish the Peronist movement with little success. Before 1983 the Radical Party won the presidency twice (in 1958 and 1963) only because the Peronist party was excluded from the elections by the armed forces who supervised them. In retaliation the labor movement protested the new governments and made it almost impossible for them to govern; consequently both of the Radical governments were judged ineffectual and were overthrown by the military before they could complete their terms. Until 1983 many in the armed forces were convinced that they were the only ones who could govern the country indefinitely.

Finally, most Argentines became notorious for resisting authentic political reform. During this century the various parties built a large national bureaucracy that they filled with their own respective patrons. Much is made of its enormity, the costs and fiscal crises that it creates, and its inadequate services. But equally troublesome is the way the millions of persons in the public and private sectors who rely on the government for their sustenance have resisted reform. They have come to expect the executive, whatever his or her ambitions, to favor little more than slight variations of the status quo. Consequently, rather than sincerely reconstruct government, those who governed either sustained or expanded it.

In 1983 the nation started over politically, but almost no one then active had experienced the pre-1930 effort to create a constitutional democracy. Instead most were nurtured on constant disruptions by authoritarian leaders who claimed that democratic government was unfeasible at the time they intervened. Anyone over the age of thirty today was socialized by repeated efforts to either rig or discard democratic political practices. They became cynical about the intent of politicians and distrustful of all but persons close to them. This does not mean that they were addicted to authoritarian politics, as some Argentines feared only a decade ago, but it does mean that the current effort to build democratic behavior must simultaneously instruct citizens on the values and conduct that it requires of them.

Few nations better illustrate the nature of common impediments and the means being employed to overcome them than Argentina currently does. A decade ago no one predicted that by 1993 Argentina would be supervised by its second consecutively elected, civilian president. Politics is changing in Argentina; however, with the changes have come new questions about how political reform should be done and what makes it succeed or fail.

Specifically, how has the conduct of Argentines affected the way institutions like the executive, legislative, and judicial branches of government operate? And what must change for these reforms to endure as more than another round in the familiar cycle that takes the nation from an authoritarian government to an elected one and then back again?

Presidential Power: Needed or Abused?

Liberal democracy was enhanced in 1983 with the Peronists' first defeat in free elections, when Radical Party candidate Raul Alfonsin beat Peronist Italo Luder. Their loss forced them to become the legitimate adversary in a constitutional system in which they had to rely on their plurality in the Senate as well as their labor movement to sustain them within the policy process. Meanwhile the armed forces, though able to stage protests against the new government over policy, could not evict it. In essence, everyone had a new role to play, and democratic government had an authentic new opportunity to function.

On the surface, political conduct after 1983 was exemplary. After President Alfonsin had received just over 50 percent of the popular vote and his Radical Party 43 percent in Congress, they went on to win a plurality in the 1985 midterm congressional elections, picking up a few more seats in the lower house. But the Peronists did not disappear. Instead, they fought back in 1987 and won their own plurality in the congressional and gubernatorial elections, setting the stage for a real comeback in the 1989 presidential elections.

It was a textbook case of incumbents lasting only until the opposition wins enough public support to evict them in free elections. And that is what Peronist Carlos Menem did when he defeated Radical Eduardo Angeloz with slightly less than a majority of the popular vote in May 1989. The Peronists played by the electoral rules while in the opposition, won a national election (though still without majority support), and were now demanding their chance to demonstrate whether they could direct a constitutional democracy. Unfortunately, the presidential transition was a bit irregular because Radical president Alfonsin was forced to resign six months ahead of schedule when the nation's descent into a hyperinflationary morass provoked demands that the transition be accelerated.

In 1989 Argentines succeeded, albeit clumsily, with their first transition between freely elected presidents since the 1920s, a major feat that in itself marked a real modification in the nation's politics. To ignore that is to deny Argentines well-deserved credit for conduct that most scholars would not have predicted a decade before. Familiar political conflicts and the socioeconomic discontent were believed to make peaceful government transitions inaccessible to Argentines. But the skeptics were proven wrong when a freely elected Peronist replaced a Radical in the presidency in 1989.

But creating a new government, however impressive, is only the first stage in the consolidation of constitutional democracy. One must still ask if this feat has led to further respect for democratic rules in government and in society, or whether it merely marked a superficial transition for which progress remains impeded by many traditional obstacles? Could the Argentine presidency become more representative and cooperative and work with a representative legislature, i.e., become less arbitrary and autonomous? And could it be done at a time when the nation was suffering its worst inflation and foreign debt ever? Many Argentine commentators expressed their doubts. To them the Argentine presidency was not prepared to change significantly from the ways its occupants had used power when they had tried to operate as pseudodictators on policy matters.[6]

To some degree the pessimists were correct. Presidents Alfonsin and Menem (more the latter than the former) did not take democratic notions of checks and balances very seriously when dealing with other branches of government. They have been especially distrustful of their legislative opposition and did as much as they could to ignore and resist it. They preferred to assign Congress the role of ratifying presidential policies and not that of fellow participants within a bargaining system of constitutionally separated authorities. Presidents have also continued to issue decrees to launch policies that Congress has opposed, always insisting that their actions were legal under emergency provisions in the Constitution.

Economic crises were often used by presidents to justify such conduct. Some bargaining with the president might be allowed now and then, especially under Alfonsin, but it was the president, not the Congress, that most people expected to lead them out of their worst economic crisis.[7] First the reluctant, ex-populist Radical president Raul Alfonsin and then Peronist president Carlos Menem in 1989 discovered the nation's desperate need for economic reconstruction and the difficulty of securing popular support for what might be harsh, regressive redistributive policies. In place of the "populist welfare state" that had characterized Argentine civilian politics previously, they were forced by the nation's huge foreign debt and record high inflation to attempt major changes in policy that affected the public and private sectors without guaranteeing anyone immediate success. In practice this meant liberalizing their economy with freer trade and the privatization of public enterprises to gain control over public finances, encourage new investment, and increase exports from all sectors.

Alfonsin reluctantly tried to make the change late in his presidency, but he failed to solve the nation's economic disarray before his 1983–1989 term ended. In fact, inflation reached record levels when his successor was elected in 1989, almost 200 percent in June alone. But Alfonsin's failure actually made it easier for Menem to justify his need for "exceptional" authority and executive autonomy. He could claim more easily than any of his predecessors that the economy required unpopular decisions and consistent policy enforcement and that only a powerful president could achieve such radical anti-inflationary objectives. And more fundamentally, he could add that the economy had not grown for almost a decade. Without an end to hyperinflation, neither Argentines nor foreigners would invest in the nation and generate the increased production and exports in a very competitive world economy, all of which Argentines needed to regain a level of affluence similar to what they had once enjoyed.

In pursuit of these objectives President Menem, especially after 1990, tried to open a tightly regulated economy and force the private sector, which had relied intensively for generations on substantial tariffs and other forms of protection and subsidization, to compete with imported goods. There was no guarantee that the public would accept the changes. Many feared the costs of such change in an industry that suddenly had to compete for the first time; in addition, millions of middle- and lower-class Argentines had relied heavily on public sector employment and social services to sustain their standard of living. Yet Menem was convinced, with the advice of the International Monetary Fund and foreign investors, that he had to make the changes using a heavy hand to accomplish what his predecessors had failed to achieve.

Not surprisingly, it led him into direct conflicts with Congress, the members of which Menem often portrayed as partisan enemies of his "sound policy," even when his own party enjoyed a plurality among senators and deputies. One of the many examples of the conflictual process was evident in the way he handled his Peronist labor movement over the issue of the "right to strike" in 1990, a controversial matter in which he found himself seeking to reduce the ability of public employees to strike so that he could implement the sale of many public enterprises to the private sector. Since 1955 different governments had tried to devise new regulations to limit strikes, but they either backed off or resorted to military repression to enforce new restrictions. Menem discovered that his effort to liberalize the Argentine economy was threatened by public sector unions who naturally feared loss of employment and power. Yet, like Juan Peron long before, Menem wanted to control labor as much as possible while he reorganized the public sector. He submitted a bill asking for authority to limit the right to strike by public sector unions, only to face a Congress that refused to act.

Menem responded to the impasse by promising to create the new law with an executive decree. Congressional leaders and the press protested his tactics, so he backed down and gave the Congress three months to review and pass his proposal. Perhaps he knew they would fail and, when they did, it would be easier to act on his own. Peronist members of Congress, with pluralities but not majorities in either house, refused to pass it once again, so after three months Menem claimed that he was giving up on Congress and decreed the new reforms.[8]

Legislative Exclusion: Avoidable or Inevitable?

The bicameral legislature has done little so far to inhibit presidential power. Nor has it achieved much public respect since it began again in 1983. It is composed of 46 senators and 254 deputies; the former are elected by provincial legislatures, and the latter by proportional representation within each province, with one-third of the seats up for election every two years. Each chamber organizes committees that normally meet in secrecy, followed by general floor sessions that are normally open to the public.

The legislature can give the appearance of being active like those in other democracies. For example, during the Alfonsin presidency (1983–1989) it passed 645 new laws. To a limited degree Congress did function, but much of the legislation passed was rudimentary and devoid of serious controversy or debate. A routine also developed in which President Alfonsin submitted bills on which he and leaders of the Peronist opposition caucus could agree secretly and in advance of submission and then quickly get them approved by a congressional vote.[9]

This resulted from initial presidential failures to secure some major changes in labor legislation that the Peronist members of Congress resisted and barely blocked. In essence, Alfonsin virtually gave up on the idea of serious legislation via Congress. The Radicals had begun in 1983 with a majority in the Chamber of Deputies but four seats less than the Peronists in the Senate. Little changed in the 1985 congressional elections, and then the Radicals lost seats in the 1987 elections, leaving President Alfonsin unable to rely on his Radical Party to secure most of the legislation that he wanted.[10]

On the legislative side the Argentine Congress is notorious for being quite "weak" institutionally. It has been noted most for being a very partisan political community that has relied on ineffectual verbal attacks within the Chamber and Senate—toward both one another and the executive branch—while devoting little time to real legislation. Such behavior was neither unusual nor hard to explain in Argentina. As one national scholar summarizes it: "The Argentine institutional system is excessively presidentialist and that discourages strategic agreements among sectors and weakens our political parties. This in turn is reflected in how little political influence has been allowed the Congress during this reestablishment of democracy in Argentina."[11]

There were other more practical obstacles as well. To staιι with, most members of Congress always bemoan their meager information about executive policies, the lack of equipment and staff within Congress for data collection, and the antiquated bureaucratization within the legislature. On their side legislators naturally blame the executive branch for some of their shortcomings. They want information about presidential proposals but claim that they seldom receive it. With their own staffs underprepared and inadequately financed to do research on their own, most legislators wander around looking lost in the process. A Peronist legislator noted that this had not changed when Menem was president. This legislator said that Congress was no more involved in serious debate than under Alfonsin, in part because "we do not know about any dangers that accompany issues like economic privatization as it occurs; we know little about the economic emergency and its management." In other words, "we are never informed." But such accusations did not offend the president; on the contrary, he merely continued to denounce "unprepared legislators" and promised to save the nation from them.[12]

Most legislators complain that they are forced to work like notary publics who merely sign documents sent over from the executive branch. Yet many in the lower ranks also criticize something popularly referred to as their own "star system" within the Senate and Chamber, whereby a few "leaders" seem more interested in their media performance than in serious argument or industrious committee work aimed at preparing real legislation within the organization. This only increases obstacles to having citizens take congressional behavior seriously. Moreover, this is not helped by the nation's reliance on proportional representation in the Chamber, which allows the parties to keep their "stars" at the top of the election lists and not give the public much chance to discard them.[13]

Ironically, congressional staffs were actually quite large when democracy was restored in 1983. Each deputy was allowed twenty-three employees and each senator ninety-eight. But here again, appearances were deceptive because most staff appointees did not work behind a desk in Buenos Aires but rather remained at home, where they devoted little of their time to legislative matters. Patronage has been the primary objective of employment in the legislative process, not hard labor for many of them. Even the members of Congress have spent most of their time back in their provinces; or, when in Buenos Aires, they devote themselves almost entirely to lobbying bureaucrats on behalf of individuals and their provincial governments.[14]

This does not mean that Congress is helpless. It can delay and even modify some legislation when the president decides to cooperate or when other members of the executive branch provide desperately needed information about legislation, but this occurs infrequently. One of the most obvious examples came in 1992, when Congress was asked to back President Menem's proposals for major reforms in the government's petroleum company (YPF) involving the sale of parts of it to private international companies. Despite some very brief but serious lobbying from the presidency in order to secure quick passage of this very important issue, President Menem and Minister of the Economy Domingo Cavallo were unable to push the privatization bill through the Chamber of Deputies as quickly as they had hoped. It was a colorful session. As the media described it, placards expressing opposition to privatization were brought in by the Radical Party members, and dissident Peronist deputies shouted "No to YPF corruption" in what turned into a carnival atmosphere with insults thrown in all directions. The attempt to consider the bill had to be abandoned when it became obvious that the president's supporters could not raise the necessary quorum, much to the chagrin of Peronists loyal to the president.

Menem immediately denounced what he liked to call the "scandalous" behavior of Congress and threatened a presidential decree, thinking it would force legislators to pass their own version of a similar bill. But his threatening the decree only enraged many in Congress.

Eventually Menem gave in some, promising some concessions to the unions in order to get the support of labor legislators in his own party. Actually, the real YPF negotiations took place not in Congress but within the executive branch, between Presidential Chief of Staff Eduardo Bauza and Argentina's labor bosses. The unions are said to have obtained a promise of a full 10 percent ownership of YPF for employees and some symbolic concessions, which finally guaranteed passage in the Congress much as Menem originally wanted.[15]

Members of Congress complained afterward of being ignored just as before. This is probably the way the president prefers it. Nose-to-nose private negotiations with the traditional centers of power—the unions in the case of the YFP, big business, the church, to a lesser extent the armed forces—are more preferable than lengthy congressional debates.[16]

Congress could change its old ways, especially if the executive branch encouraged it, but presidents prefer to guard their traditional power over the legislative process. This leaves Argentina with a Congress that is known in the popular press for (1) political debates that are notorious for their incomprehensible political jargon and (2) arguments that are characterized by a verbal perniciousness rather than serious refutations of positions. Scandals among a few legislators, as well as extreme factionalism (especially among the Peronists), have also hurt congressional credibility. Consequently, most citizens believe that they cannot communicate with legislators without becoming members of what they perceive to be an elitist class.[17]

Congress does have its defenders. As one Argentine political analyst argues, Congress is as much a victim of excessive demands on it by its most outspoken critics as it is the source of its own problems. He insists:

> It is true that many deputies do not work, do not attend sessions, lose time with empty discussions, that committees are slow, and that many times they vote for laws without sufficient analysis. But, more than that, there is another face of truth in all this: the Congress is facing much demand from society, a level of expectation that it cannot satisfy. It has no way to respond to these demands. These demands involve a desire that the major problems that face us be dealt with, leaving everyone content. That is impossible. The Congress has many functions. In order to make a law one must achieve a compromise among very diverse opinions and points of view; without agreements there are no laws many times. Voting for a law is not just going into a session and raising one's hand. There are deputies with little prestige among the public who are really hard workers, who are conscientious and many times are an important factor in decisions.[18]

He urges Argentines to recalculate their expectations because they are habitually too impatient in judging Congress and because their cynical, contentious attitudes do not really achieve anything. What they must do to improve Congress is cease abusing it, he insists. Instead they must behave like democratic citizens seeking better representation by calling legislators, writing them, pressuring them, and helping them in order for them to feel responsible and obligated to account for themselves.

Equally important, some citizens have begun to debate the meaning of political representation. They understand that modern democracy is supposed to be "representative democracy," and that no perfect system of representation exists. But even though members of the Senate are chosen by provincial legislatures and those in the national Chamber of Deputies are chosen through the D'Hondt system of proportional representation—an approach that has traditionally been regarded as very representative because it distributes seats by province in proportion to the votes received by each party—some citizens ask if this is really the best way.

Proportional representation itself is being called into question, with some persons going so far as to demand it be replaced with a single-member district system much like the one used by the House of Representatives in the United States. They complain that proportional representation has allowed party leaders to draw up lists of candidates in each province that are filled by members of party elites who are more attentive to their immediate political peers than to the people whom they are supposed to represent in the province. Critics of this system insist that they want to know and influence candidates, and they believe that a single-member district system with party primary elections would give party members and the general electorate a better chance to select whom they wish. They are not worried at this point about any of the adverse effects of such a system on minor parties or its tendency to favor incumbents over challengers. They are more eager to break up the control exercised by party elites.

Obviously, changing the rules will not, by itself, make Argentine democracy truly representative. That must be done through practice. Moreover, single-member district representation may give enormous advantage to the party with pluralities in the most districts—currently the Peronists—which is hardly the objective of those who support the change. Nevertheless, advocates want to break the old system before concerning themselves with possible difficulties that might follow reform. In the 1991 and 1993 congressional elections the electorate still operated under D'Hondt, but that did not deter it from selecting some candidates who were younger, less devoted to a political party, and more committed (at least verbally) to being responsive to their provincial constituents.

Nothing is simple in Argentine politics, however. Strong presidential power to deal with economic problems was only part of the equation. Equally important to presidents is their desire to revise the Constitution in order to permit themselves to remain in office longer than is currently permitted. The Argentine Constitution limits the president to a single, six-year term. Yet during this latest phase of democracy both incumbents have tried to alter the Constitution during their first term in order to allow them to run for a second one. Alfonsin entertained the idea of constitutional reforms to permit either his reelection as president or his election to a new role such as prime minister. But when he did, his party lost badly in the 1987 congressional elections and the matter ended. Yet this did not stop

Menem from calling for a constitutional amendment that would permit him to pursue reelection after his term expires in 1995.

This is why public and media attention focused on congressional
elections in early October 1993. Menem needed congressional cooperation because he sought to enhance his authority through the proposed constitutional amendment. In addition, he wanted to have the
president elected directly, replacing the nation's electoral college, and
to shorten the presidential term from six to four years. To accomplish
this he would need a two-thirds vote in both houses of Congress. In the
Senate the Peronists were just one seat short of a majority as the elections approached, but they were fifty-four short in the Chamber of
Deputies. Even though half of the Chamber seats would be up, no one
believed that the Peronists would manage a majority of the seats. To
amend the Constitution, then, they would have to use members of
small regional parties and some Radicals in the Chamber of
Deputies.[19]

Menem also had to contend with the General Federation of Labor
(CGT) movement, whose leaders refused to declare themselves for his
reelection until he paid a hefty price to them. Essentially they demand-
ed (1) the repeal of the decree linking pay raises to increases in pro-
ductivity and (2) the postponement of the reform of the rules that governed *obras sociales,* the government's social security funds that totaled
$3.5 billion and were managed by the unions. But Menem refused to
concede initially. So when polls were taken during the several months
before the election in 1993, they showed real division in the electorate, with only 27 percent favoring reelection of the incumbent,
even though many more approved of some amendment allowing presidents to be elected twice in the future.[20]

Menem was not helped by the fact that Minister of the Interior
Gustavo Beliz resigned on August 23, 1993, or by protesting senior officials who were "generating an unacceptable state of suspicion" by the
way they were trying to further Menem's reelection goal. Beliz also
claimed that some of the president's aides were prepared to buy opposition votes in an effort to secure the needed two-thirds majority in
both houses of Congress.[21]

Menem and others insisted that continuity was essential for maintaining Menem's liberal economic reforms. This argument always has
some merit in a nation like Argentina, where policy reversals or anticipation of them have often undermined policy. To his credit Menem
avoided this problem by holding firm to his economic policies during
the first few years of his administration. As a result his government
took the annual triple-digit inflation rate and brought it down to 84

percent in 1991 and just 17.5 percent in 1992. It was a major achievement.[22]

Argentines did pay a high price for it, though, because Menem pegged Argentine currency to the U.S. dollar in 1991, which denied consumers one of the ways to play the foreign exchange game that often saved them from losing real personal wealth. Everything became more expensive in Argentina after 1991, and wages did not keep pace. Retired persons and the growing lower class suffered the most but were told that they had little choice but to stick with current policy if the economy was to continue its stabilization and expansion. It left many Argentines to wonder if their days of relative affluence were long behind them.

This also confronted the Argentine electorate with a difficult political dilemma: Was the incumbent president like a dike whose consistent economic policies had prevented a flood of policy changes that might undermine economic liberalization and recovery? Or were there others among them who now understood what was required and were in the 1990s as able as the incumbent to avert a return to economic chaos? In other words, were Argentines ready to find and elect someone else who could govern as well or better than the presidential incumbent? Polls showed that the people remained divided in 1993 over whether changing the president was worth the risk, though a majority continued to favor giving change a try.[23]

Then came the legislative elections on October 3, 1993. Would it be another debacle for the president, as happened in 1987 when Alfonsin's Radicals lost badly in their second congressional election, or would Menem and the Peronistas hold on and increase his chances of constitutional reform? As it turned out, Menem was pleased with the results.

Unlike Alfonsin and his Radicals, who were defeated in their second by-election in 1987, the Peronists picked up more seats in 1993 by taking 42 percent of the total vote, going from 116 to 125 of the Chamber's total of 257. Meanwhile the Radicals, with 30 percent of the vote, stayed the same, with 84 seats. The remaining 48 seats were divided among twenty minor parties. Equally as surprising as this increase in total votes was the Peronist victory in the city of Buenos Aires, which had long been a Radical Party stronghold. The Peronist ballot list was led by Erman Gonzalez, who had once served as Menem's minister of economics and later as defense minister. With an increasing number of people in the Chamber who had worked with Menem, some speculated that he might try to work more closely with Congress. The issue would be over the Chamber's new role: it could become a rubber stamp led by presidential allies in a virtual parliamentary style of politics, or it might be a body with which the president was willing to play a real game of bargaining.[24]

The Peronist triumph encouraged Menem to begin another campaign for amending the Constitution, but there was no guarantee that he would succeed. The election results left the Peronists with substantially less than the two-thirds of the seats in both houses of Congress that they needed for passing amendments. Menem would still have to rely on some votes from a few Radicals as well as the usual support he had received from minor regional parties. And to get that he would have to overcome his critics, who continued to fear that his reelection would turn the nation's politics even more into its subjugation by an excessive concentration of presidential power.

In 1993 it was not the idea of being governed by another Peronist president that worried Argentines. Menem had reduced old fears on everything but the corruption issue. What concerned the public was a return to the monopolization of power by one person who refused to leave office, much as happened under Juan Peron and other presidents. Few objected to Menem completing his term as scheduled, but public opinion remained very divided over whether that entitled him to change the rules for himself rather than only for his successors.

Conclusion

No one had expected the Argentine Congress to become a powerful branch of government immediately in a nation accustomed to being dominated by its president. Nor did the hyperinflation that consumed the country in the late 1980s breed any desire to rely more than before on anything but a civilian executive branch to rescue the nation. Most Argentines, when they began to rebuild democracy in 1983, expected Congress to become a place for the dominant political parties to deposit some of their members in the hope that they would gradually learn how to legislate productively. In the meantime the public wanted inflation ended and their self-confidence as a nation increased by their president.

Congress was never closed nor totally ignored. It could debate major issues, especially when the president occasionally realized that its inclusion in his policymaking was needed to generate more popular support for his programs. Some in the presidential office even went so far in 1992 as to submit the presidential budget to Congress before it had been implemented, for the first time in nearly fifty years. But this was the exception, not the rule, in presidential-congressional relations.

Clearly it would be naive to conclude that Argentina is well on its way to making democratic government work. One can acknowledge and even applaud its progress with civil liberties and elections without pretending that the process is completed. Argentines must still decide if they really want a legislative process for anything but the ratification of executive leadership. The citizens must also decide what it will take to equip legislators to do their job and how their performance should be assessed. Maybe the best that the Argentine people can hope for currently is a marginal role that prohibits unrestricted presidential domination, but even that is not clear at the moment. It has been more common for the Congress to appear insincere to the public and incapable of sustaining serious debate leading to concrete legislation. And naturally the executive, with its power of decree, did little to discourage such opinion.

Equally important, but often ignored in explaining the legislature's inability to restrict presidential power, is the failure of the nation's judiciary to implement anything resembling checks and balances within the national government. President Menem's first attempt to reform the judicial system was not aimed at improving its operation, but instead was a very self-serving attempt to increase the size of the Supreme Court. He rushed through Congress a bill that added four new positions to the five-member court, and then in one day filled them with judges supporting his new government. When the process was finished, the result was a rather docile Menem court that gave him no trouble with his use of presidential authority thereafter. This left the public quite cynical about the constitutional court and its ability to limit authorities who abuse the Constitution.

Argentines are vulnerable to potential presidential abuse of authority and to insincere leadership. But they also remember how quickly they can descend into political conflict and economic collapse if their government leadership does not succeed with reasonable policies. And that should work to the president's advantage, for as long as the fear of failure remains, Argentines are likely to be wary of thoroughgoing reform of the policy process until they know that all branches can behave reliably. Despite their woes the Argentines are not naive about what they are going through or about the difficulty of making it succeed. They also seem to agree that despite the new system's faults, it remains preferable to the military, authoritarian way of governing that they have sincerely cast aside.

Notes

1. For a summary of the region's authoritarian political culture, see Howard Wiarda, "Toward a Framework for the Study of Political Changes in the Iberic-Latin Tradition: The Corporative Model," *World Politics* (January 1973), pp. 206–235, and many others.

2. See Terri Lynn Karl, "Dilemmas of Democratization in Latin America," *Comparative Politics,* Vol. 23 (October 1990), pp. 1–23.

3. See Robert Dahl, *Polyarchy* (New Haven: Yale University Press, 1976).

4. Robert Dahl, *Polyarchy;* and Adam Przeworski, *Democracy and the Market* (Cambridge: Cambridge University Press, 1991).

5. See Gary W. Wynia, *Argentina: Illusions and Realities* (New York: Holmes and Meier, 1992).

6. See James Neilson, *Noticias,* April 22, 1990, p. 39, on these practices.

7. Atilio Cadorin, *La Nacion,* June 17, 1990, p. 9.

8. See Eduardo L. Bonelli, *La Nacion,* March 22, 1990, section 3, p. 2.

9. M. Mustapic and Matteo Goretti, "Gobierno y Oposicion en el Congreso: La Practica de la Presidencia de Alfonsin (1983–1989)," Di Tella Institute Paper (Buenos Aires: Instituto Di Tella, 1991).

10. See Gary W. Wynia, *Argentina: Illusions and Realities,* 2d edition (New York: Holmes and Meier, 1992), Chapter 7.

11. Jesus Rodriguez, "La Democracia Argentina Diez Anos Despues: Nuevas Prioridades," paper delivered at the Latin American Program, The Woodrow Wilson Center, The Smithsonian Institute, Washington, D.C., March 6, 1993, p. 7.

12. Atilio Cadorin, *La Nacion,* June 24, 1990, p. 9.

13. See Holger Bunning, *Noticias de la Fundacion Arturo Illia,* cuatro trimestre de 1989, No. 8, pp. 39–40.

14. *La Nacion,* March 15, 1990, p. 12.

15. *Buenos Aires Herald,* September 27, 1992, p. 2.

16. A summary of the congressional-presidential battle over the YPF bill can be found in *Buenos Aires Herald,* September 27, 1992, p. 2.

17. Holger Bunning, *Noticias,* pp. 39–40.

18. Manuel Mora y Araujo, *Poder Ciudadano,* Vol. 1, No. 4 (1990), p. 10.

19. *Latin American Weekly Report,* March 11, 1993, p. 2.

20. Ibid., p. 3.

21. *Latin American Weekly Report,* September 23, 1993, p. 434.

22. *Economist,* January 16, 1993, p. 46.

23. For an insightful essay on these dilemmas, see Juan Carlos Torre, "Some Thoughts on the Relationship Between Political Liberalization and Economic Liberalization in the Light of the Argentine Experience," paper delivered at The Woodrow Wilson Center, The Smithsonian Institute, April 6, 1993, p. 11.

24. *Clarin,* October 4, 1993, pp. 1–4. Also see *New York Times,* October 5, 1993, p. A8.

5

The Legislature and Democratic Transition in Brazil

Daniel Zirker

It is a special weakness of social science that its analytic lens does not usually focus upon specific institutions until they have already emerged as critical actors in society. As Hegel put it, "the Owl of Minerva spreads its wings only with the falling of dusk." The ground-breaking works of the late 1960s and early 1970s that explored the role of the military in authoritarian systems,[1] for example, appeared in many cases a decade after the political reemergence of that institution in so many countries. Today, as the uneven and fragile worldwide movement toward democratization—the "third wave" as Samuel P. Huntington refers to it[2]—has marked a decade, studies of the institutional underpinnings of democracy are only recently appearing with any frequency.

Political parties, elections, the dynamics of representation, and especially legislatures are obviously of central interest in understanding the growth and maintenance of democratic tendencies in developing countries. Nevertheless, the role of legislatures is far less clear, and far more changeable, than was that of the military establishments in the authoritarian regimes in Latin America and Southern Europe in the 1960s. This relates directly to the complexity and sensitivity of democratization and democracy. There is, moreover, a related concern: the vulnerability of such institutions to socioeconomic and political disorder. Authoritarian impulses are usually spearheaded by democracy's alter ego, demagoguery. The fostering of strong and vibrant institutions is the only adequate defense against the caducity of democracy.

Brazil has always been a country of extraordinarily weak institutions and, occasionally at least, strong political personalities. The two consistently strongest institutions have been the military and the Roman Catholic Church; among the weakest and most ephemeral have been political parties, with the possible recent exception of the

Workers' Party (PT).[3] The perennial weakness of Brazilian political parties constitutes a severe impediment to Brazilian democratization. Political parties are crucial elements in the maintenance of strong and dynamic legislatures.[4] Although Alfred Stepan argued in 1971 that the Brazilian National Congress "has been one of the strongest in Latin America in this century," he also noted that its principal activities were the distribution of resources to regional interests and, very significantly, the blocking of reforms.[5]

By most accounts, the National Congress has seldom had very much popular legitimacy,[6] tending to function, rather, as a vehicle for elite interest articulation and accommodation.[7] As Scott Mainwaring observes, party affiliation, a key basis of democratic representation, has little impact in structuring the popular vote for politicians in Brazil, and hence most representatives pay little attention to party positions.[8] He concludes that "there is probably no other democracy that grants politicians so much autonomy vis-à-vis their parties. This [Brazilian] electoral and party legislation in turn reinforces the individualistic behavior of politicians."[9] Regional cleavages also contribute to a situation in which major politicians "prefer legislation that enhances their autonomy at the expense of weakening parties."[10]

The powerful position of the Brazilian president, moreover, particularly in dispensing patronage, has frequently precluded any meaningful political challenges to him by members of Congress. The three Brazilian presidents since the end of the military dictatorship in 1985 have had to build support bases by working directly against the strength of political parties.[11] That this has succeeded in most instances reinforces the common view of Brazil as a president-centered political system.[12] The likely role of the National Congress in the Brazilian democratization process that was initiated with the *abertura* (political opening) after 1979, therefore, was predictably not propitious; very few serious studies have examined the Congress during the past decade.[13]

The Congress has contributed only episodically and unevenly to the process of democratization in Brazil. It has tended to act dynamically in this regard only during national political crises, and specifically when such crises have led to popular mobilization and direct public scrutiny of legislative behavior. Nevertheless, its adaptation as a forum for the expression of opposition to executive largesse has lent to it an aura of mass politics and democracy, despite its often profoundly elitist and antidemocratic behavior. Hence the legislature continues to be a confusing and complicated piece in the Brazilian democratization puzzle.

Six recent congressional periods and institutional adaptations stand out as formative in understanding this complex role:

1. the nadir of dictatorship, 1965–1974, when the Congress served as a key source of legitimation and system maintenance;
2. the period 1974–1980, during which the Congress's role as an opposition to the dictatorship evolved;
3. the legislature's audible, if ineffectual, response to mass calls for direct presidential elections in the early 1980s (and its subsequent role as a presidential electoral college);
4. its role as a constitutional convention in 1987–1988;
5. its reluctant impeachment of President Fernando Collor de Mello in 1992;
6. the dramatic corruption scandal that engulfed it beginning in October 1993.

The development of a unique legislative culture, particularly during the first two periods, explains the persistence of such a conservative legislature in Brazil during an era of rapid democratization.

The traditional political norms and membership of the Brazilian Congress have been frankly elitist and, over the past twenty years, frequently alienating to both the poor and relatively wealthy parts of "Belindia," as Brazil is sometimes called.[14] Although, as Daniel Levy notes, "democracy often begins with public contestation restricted to certain groups,"[15] the weak and amorphous character of Brazilian political parties, the blatant coopting of elections by self-interested elites, and the common association of elite-centered corruption with political office have all contributed to a "crisis of representation," in which "the strongest links between citizens and their representative institutions are dissolving or are proving difficult to forge."[16] One of the structural bases of this crisis, the proportional representation system by which members of the Chamber of Deputies are chosen, appears to have been designed specifically to weaken, rather than strengthen, the legislature. Moreover, a series of laws and "packages," many of them promulgated by military dictatorial decree, sought to prevent specific electoral and legislative outcomes and especially the emergence of the opposition as a majority.[17] These unfortunately appear to have had a formative effect on subsequent legislative behavior.

The Brazilian legislature's contribution to democracy was frankly and actively suppressed by military and political elites. It was forced into a "bipartist" mode, and hence remained suspect in the eyes of most Brazilians by the early 1970s.[18] Douglas Chalmers has argued that the effective building of democratic institutions in Latin America requires that three critical concerns be addressed: restraining the prince; empowering the weak; and disciplining the powerful.[19] As a passive agent of legitimation during much of the past two decades, the Brazilian Congress has shown little enthusiasm for these roles. Nevertheless, as an examination of the following key congressional roles and episodes demonstrates, popular reaction has increasingly pressured the institution such that its passive elite facade is now visibly crumbling. The obvious worry is that a complete collapse of its most elite-oriented and antidemocratic elements may ultimately preclude the emergence of a stronger, more democratic institution in its place. Military intervention and executive absolutism have been common Brazilian responses to legislative weakness in the past.

The Congress as an Agent of Legitimacy for the Dictatorship

The Brazilian National Congress was largely molded in its current and distinctive form during the twenty-one-year military dictatorship that began on March 31, 1964.[20] A profound disdain was evinced by the dictatorship toward the Congress: previously existing political parties were summarily abolished and replaced with two official parties; the legislature suffered repeated arbitrary closures by military presidents; and presidential rule by decree and the direct use of coercion against legislators became the norm. Nevertheless, as Thomas E. Skidmore notes, "the very fact that the government which came to power in 1964 found it necessary to purge the congress repeatedly and eventually to close it despite these purges shows that these authoritarian leaders feared 'interference' in policy making."[21]

The Congress was systematically weakened as a legislative body,[22] and it was forced into a distinctively episodic, legitimizing role that persisted after 1985, when the military formally handed over power to a civilian president. This political transition, moreover, was not the direct product of mass mobilization, although important instances of spontaneous mobilization in opposition to the dictatorship occurred after 1978. It was, rather, primarily the result of a rather traditional process of elite accommodation.[23] Nevertheless, the visible presence of the Congress as a legitimizing agent remained important to the dictatorship, given its "extremely precarious support" from the national bourgeoisie.[24]

Four descriptive and interrelated characteristics of the Congress became hardened during the nadir of dictatorship and relate directly to the institution's impotence and cooptation during this and subsequent periods. The first of these might be labeled *converse representation*. Simply stated, this is the manipulation of voters through regional and local politics to ensure a given electoral outcome. In this pattern, the interests of a narrow elite are ultimately reinforced (or perhaps represented) by large, controlled voting blocs that periodically and obediently legitimate the "system." Though it is tied (during elections, at least) to the limited distribution of federal resources, such converse representation makes no real attempt to represent the interests of the electorate; rather, it appears to be the bizarre reinforcing of the long-term interests of a narrow economic and political elite by well-behaved mass voting blocs.[25] As Philippe Schmitter demonstrates, legitimate interest groups during the dictatorship quickly recognized how little the legislature engaged in delegate representation, and they focused their energies away from the Congress.[26] Such manipulation had regional implications, with representatives from the more developed regions apparently less prone to such behavior,[27] and hence much more closely associated with conventional models of representation.

The second characteristic of the Brazilian legislature during the military dictatorship that has endured after 1985 is that of *opposition posturing* for direct (individual) political gain. This is, in essence, political opposition as a soapbox activity,[28] and it was particularly evident in the mid-1970s, when the official opposition party, the Brazilian Democratic Movement (MDB), began to serve as a queue for presidential hopefuls.

The military dictatorship consistently underestimated the depth and breadth of the more pervasive and dynamic opposition expressed by the voters of Brazil, and hence, as Skidmore notes, "any two-party race at this time inevitably turned into a plebiscite on the government."[29] Nevertheless, no real policy opposition on the part of civilian institutions was possible,[30] and opposition posturing actually aided the dictatorship to the extent that it imparted upon the Congress an aura of legitimacy while reinforcing passive legislative behavior.

The third characteristic was a frequent, if somewhat reluctant, institutional focus upon *limited crisis management* during challenges to elite governance in Brazil. This pattern tended to occur after broadly popular/mobilizing issues had first resulted in the posturing of members of Congress and then, only secondarily, sometimes resulted in the passage of measures that addressed these broad-based mass concerns, usually in the interests of preserving order. Examples of this during the dictatorship included congressional responses to the executive political banning (*cassação*) of key political figures, including individual members of Congress; congressional responses to arbitrary changes by the military of the electoral rules; and responses to egregious human rights violations.

The fourth pattern was that of *passive acquiescence to overt cooptation.* Members of the National Congress became critically dependent upon the military-dominated executive branch for the distribution of resources. Virtually all legislators became subject to executive discipline through the withholding of these resources, such that by the end of the dictatorship, a state governor from the progovernment Social Democratic Party (PDS) who displeased President (and General) João Baptista Figueiredo was compelled to seek the intercession of an opposition congressional deputy on his behalf, under publicly demeaning circumstances, in order to secure normal federal funding for his state. During the first civilian presidency of José Sarney, as many as fifty legislators per week were visiting the minister of the army *in his barracks office,* frenetically attempting to secure his support in gaining resources.[31] Hence, although Elio Gaspari has recently accused some members of the Workers' Party of beginning to act like *vivandeiras* (women who followed armies around in the eighteenth and nineteenth centuries), because of their attempts to appeal to the military establishment during the 1993 corruption scandal,[32] congressional dependence upon military politics is nothing new. Such political dependence apparently contributed to the emergence within Congress of an ambivalent and confused self-image by the 1990s.

These four patterns, then, should be seen in the context of (1) decidedly limited congressional defiance of the dictatorship and (2) the effects upon the legislature of subsequent dictatorial retaliation. Although the initial response of many politicians, including members of Congress, to the 1964 intervention was to attempt to utilize it to further their own political interests,[33] the military quickly and effectively asserted itself. Less than a week after the overthrow of President João Goulart, Congress was requested by the military to formalize its removal of the political rights of dozens of civilian politicians, including many of its own members.[34] Ignoring a congressional emergency act, the military issued its first "institutional act," drafted by Francisco Campos. Campos was the authoritarian author of the 1937 New State Constitution,[35] which could be described in its own terms as the basis upon which the 1964 coup had become an institutionalized "revolution."[36] The National Congress was now described as having derived its legitimacy from this institutional act, which required the national legislature to extend sweeping powers to the executive.[37] Numerous subsequent institutional acts would further weaken the Congress. When the legislature defied executive authority, moreover, as in its refusal in 1969 to censure Deputy Marcio Moreira Alves, consequent military institutional decrees specified measures for disciplining the institution, including (as in the Alves case) its indefinite suspension.[38]

Open defiance of the executive by the legislature was thus systematically minimized, although key ideologues of the dictatorship, including General Golbery do Couto e Silva, consistently held that maintenance of order by the dictatorship vitally depended upon maintaining a liberalizing constitutional system.[39] As Robert Kaufman observes, this increasingly allowed members of Congress, along with journalists and academics, to test the parameters of the system, "pressing with varying degrees of militance for greater legislative autonomy, a larger role for the parties, more freedom in the press and the universities, more opportunities for debate within the electoral arena."[40] It also allowed the legislature to become a forum for the establishment of *pactos sociais*—elite social pacts capable of limited representation of (and thereby limiting the political impact of) mass political demands.

Crucial to the continued docile and elite character of the National Congress was the unique proportional representation system that originated well before the 1964 intervention but was maintained and revised during the dictatorship. It was based upon the D'Hondt formula of 1950, which divides the number of votes (both valid and blank) in each state by the number of seats in the Chamber of Deputies for that state. Unlike other proportional systems, individual candidates are listed on the ballot; however, if a given candidate is not elected, his or her votes are added to the total party votes and can be used to elect another candidate in that party. As Amaury de Souza observes, this encourages parties to submit the largest possible number of candidates, "the majority of whom have a minimal chance of being elected."[41] Given the chronic weakness and malleability of political parties in Brazil, this adaptation of proportional representation has provided an ideal means of maintaining a legislature principally representative of the economic and political elite, and hence containing popular mobilization.

The 1967 Constitution provided additional machinery for authoritarian control over the legislature. By establishing a system dominated by loyal-party politics and characterized by weak congressional party leaders who were dependent upon the military, the military command hoped to maintain the Congress as an effective agent of legitimation and an ineffective institutional opponent.[42] The sublegenda law of 1968 further entrenched this system by allowing parties to submit up to three candidates *under the same party label* for a single position of mayor or senator. The candidate with the most votes from the party with the most votes won. This united the progovernment ARENA Party, allowing it to stifle its fractionalizing tendencies.[43]

The official opposition party, the MDB, soon benefited from the salutary effects of the military's pro-ARENA legislation, however. By the early 1970s, the MDB, which had come to represent the industrialized South and Southeast of Brazil, was exerting far more pressure on the dictatorship than had been envisioned. The dictatorship, in turn, was becoming increasingly dependent on legislative support from the impoverished Northeast, a region long dominated by the political machines of large landowners. This pattern would continue to intensify throughout the dictatorship.

Congress and the Abertura, 1978–1982

Military concerns with the nemesis of dictatorship, the inevitable erosion of the dictatorship's legitimacy, and the growing resentment among the national economic elites of military rule contributed to a gradual easing of political repression that eventually came to be known as the abertura. Elite civilian bickering after the *golpe* had quickly degenerated into serious fractionalization of progovernment parties, as well as the creation of the official two-party system in 1965, followed deliberations in which the military authorities even considered attempting to implement a Mexican-style single-party system to guarantee its long-term political hegemony.[44]

Pressures for economic growth and a technocratic aversion to political conflict profoundly affected the legislature. Skidmore refers to the legislature as of 1971 as "a compliant façade of a congress, shorn of any independent powers."[45] Nevertheless, as Robert Packenham's argument from the same period goes, the Congress retained two important, if sporadically employed, functions that related to elite mediation: it was a potential "safety valve," allowing for the abatement of acute political tensions; and it was capable of performing what Packenham calls the "exit function," the resolution of an impasse among national elites.[46] Hence, although the National Congress was periodically closed down by the dictatorship,[47] it was predictably reopened and tolerated as an unwieldy but necessary tool of the executive.[48]

The military was itself beset by fractionalization, including the emergence of the *linha dura*, or hard-line authoritarian nationalists, who periodically threatened dominant "internationalist" ideologues such as General Golbery do Couto e Silva.[49] Furthermore, the effects of the authoritarian period that accompanied the "Brazilian economic miracle"—which began with Institutional Act 5 and the authoritarian crackdown of December 1968, and included high growth rates with low income redistribution—were increasingly seen as undermining the regime's legitimacy. As President (and General) Médici was said to have put it during the "economic miracle" of the early 1970s, "Brazil is doing well, the people are doing badly."

By 1973 Golbery and his successor General Geisel had become sufficiently concerned about the perceived crisis of legitimation that they began exploring a possible political détente.[50] The legislature naturally dominated these concerns, particularly after the striking gains by the MDB in the 1974 elections and the increasing interest of the MDB in labor policies. The rapid growth of unionization, partly the product of the industrialization of the "Brazilian miracle," and also the result of decaying authoritarianism, gave the MDB an expanding and highly organized constituency. Votes after 1975 on social issues such as the legalization of divorce likewise contributed to what Skidmore calls the "relegitimization" of the legislature.[51] The Congress's new legitimacy contributed in turn to the legitimacy of the system. Growing legislative opposition to the regime thus ironically became an important tool for regime maintenance.[52]

The trick, of course, was to manage that legislative opposition, allowing it to legitimize the system while delaying its ultimate victory—the wresting by a civilian elite of political power from the military hierarchy—as long as possible. The dictatorship relied heavily in this on the cooperation of the progovernment party leaders, who fought for the president's agenda in exchange for personal political and economic rewards.[53] By 1978, the use of delaying tactics by the dictatorship was becoming increasingly expensive, however. Labor union activity had boiled over into major strikes, notably on behalf of the metalworkers; the MDB was increasingly unified and coherent in its opposition; and the middle class was increasingly disillusioned with military dictatorship.

As General Figueiredo prepared to take over the presidency in 1979, the Congress had become an immediate threat to continuing military dictatorship in Brazil. Passage of the Falcão Law, which drastically limited opposition candidates' access to the media, and the April Package, which created appointed senators (humorously dubbed "bionic senators" by the media) and increased the number of deputies from the Northeast, ensured a favorable outcome for the military in the congressional elections of 1978; at the same time, a general political amnesty law guaranteed that there would be no "revanchism" against the torturers associated with the dictatorship. Hence, the government's ARENA Party gained a 231 to 189 majority in the Chamber of Deputies, though it had a popular vote margin of only 250,000 out of 38 million votes and was now almost completely dependent upon the rural political machines in underdeveloped regions such as the Northeast. In the populous, industrial South and Center-South, the government party had been buried in a landslide. In the Senate, it had managed to reinforce its majority, taking a 42 to 24 majority, while losing the popular vote 43 percent to 57 percent to the MDB.[54] Shortly thereafter the government abolished the official two-party system, and the newly metamorphosed MDB, now the Party of the MDB (PMDB), quickly lost ground to a number of new opposition parties. Most of the ARENA membership, meanwhile, adhered to the new Social Democratic Party. Not surprisingly, the subsequent proliferation of parties was cited by a Brazilian social scientist in 1993 as a critical barrier to democracy.[55]

The military's temporarily renewed mandate in the late 1970s was soon complicated by a series of events, and the Congress was again used—at some cost to the military—to legitimize dictatorship. A repressive law concerning foreigners in 1980, an abortive attempt by remnants of the repressive security apparatus to bomb a folk concert in Rio de Janeiro in 1981, the assassination by hard-line officers of a right-wing journalist who had learned too much about the Brazilian nuclear weapons program, and several other less prominent human rights violations increasingly focused attention upon the 1982 congressional and gubernatorial elections. The dictatorship attempted to pad its margin of victory with (1) a new "linked voting" requirement that forced electors to vote a straight ticket and (2) a constitutional amendment that added further to representation of the Northeast in the Chamber of Deputies and the electoral college (which was scheduled to choose the new president in 1984).[56]

Although the elections resulted in a continued PDS majority in the Senate, a plurality in the Chamber of Deputies, and a slight majority in the electoral college, the governorships of the industrialized states were swept by opposition candidates. General Figueiredo's heart attack in 1982 further complicated military dominance over the legislature. The Congress was centrally featured in the news media as an arbiter of change and a single important source of legitimacy. This was especially evident in the high public standing of the long-term leader of the opposition in the legislature, Ulysses Guimarães, a strident voice against dictatorship whose reputation for honesty and sincerity had apparently put him beyond the reach of military sanctions.[57] Nevertheless, the National Congress remained a manipulatory and manipulated body of political elites. The new political parties lacked, for the most part,[58] any institutional structure or ideological consistency, preferring to focus upon charismatic personalities, to manipulate voting blocs, and to serve as vehicles for furthering individual political careers. Mass politics remained notably absent from the new political equation.

Diretas Já! and Presidential Selection, 1982–1985

The Diretas Já! campaign, a mass-based attempt to bring about direct elections for the presidency, injected mass popular protest into the elitist military/congressional formula for the transition to civilian government. As a key PT platform plank in 1983, and based upon a proposed constitutional amendment that had been quietly introduced in the Congress by PMDB deputy Dante de Oliveira, the call for direct elections represented a wildly popular opposition issue. By January 1984, the PMDB had thrown its weight behind the campaign, and millions of demonstrators filled the streets of Rio de Janeiro and São Paulo.

As the campaign gathered broad-based popular support, drawing the largest demonstrations in Brazilian history, it was also discovered by the news media.[59] Nevertheless, true to its elite composition and disposition, the Congress, with the accession of the PMDB, soon manipulated and limited the campaign. By the April congressional vote on the amendment, which was twenty-two votes short of the required two-thirds majority in the Chamber of Deputies, the legislators evinced a palpable fear that continued street demonstrations would lead to a breakdown of order and further military intervention. A coalition of convenience between civilian and military elites had once again won the day despite the PT's attractive call for street demonstrations to continue until a direct election was held.[60] Despite its failure in the short term, however, the carnival-like explosion of political participation in Diretas Já! had a lasting impact on mass politics in Brazil.

Of particular interest was the way in which the Diretas Já! campaign organizers had focused popular attention upon specific legislative behavior. Organizers in each state placed large placards at the ready so that each legislator's vote could be immediately publicized. Legislators found themselves in an unaccustomed situation—they were being pressured to vote as representatives; the public, moreover, tangibly affected a key political outcome through mass protests and the publicizing of legislators' votes. The government of General Figueiredo was not alone in its awkward and unsupportive response to these developments. The Congress was also visibly uncomfortable with this outburst of democratic sentiment during what seemed to be accepted by civilian and military elites as a controlled, gradual, and elite-oriented return to civilian rule.

The congressional defeat of the amendment for direct elections in 1984 determined that the constitutionally provided electoral college, composed of the members of the Congress along with delegates chosen from state legislatures and municipal councils, would elect the first civilian president in twenty-one years. Given the favorable representation from the conservative Northeast, where old-fashioned machine politics are still the rule, the dictatorship's control over the selected delegates, and the existence of the "bionic" (appointed) senators, the 686 members of the electoral college could be expected under reasonable conditions to confirm the government party's candidate. As Stepan has argued, had it not been for the coalescing of the following three highly unlikely conditions, an opposition candidate could not have succeeded. These conditions were as follows: (1) an opposition candidate capable of bringing some government party members into the opposition had to win the opposition's nomination; (2) that candidate had to have the ability to unite the opposition while attracting government party votes; and (3) the military had to allow a divisive and relatively unpopular candidate to be nominated by the government party.[61] The nominations of the widely popular centrist Tancredo Neves by the opposition and of Paulo Maluf (a divisive and manipulatory machine politician) by the PDS ultimately determined that an opposition candidate would be selected in early 1985. However, despite his political advantages, Neves campaigned hard among the PDS electors and was even advised by one of his opponent's former campaign managers to visit the families of every member of the electoral college; this advisor reportedly said, "If an elector passes by Tancredo and is not recognized, [Tancredo's vote] is lost. Anyone who thinks that these little courtesies are not important does not understand indirect election."[62]

The elite character of the electoral process remained intact despite Tancredo's victory in the electoral college in January 1985. Furthermore, Tancredo fell ill the night before his inauguration (March 15, 1985) and deteriorated rapidly, dying in a hospital just over a month later. His running mate, José Sarney, who had been the government party leader in the Chamber of Deputies prior to a belated conversion to the opposition, became president. The Sarney presidency was clearly a transitional phase, with the military ministers playing a fundamentally conservatizing role, particularly as far as the drafting of the 1988 Constitution was concerned.

The Legislature as Constitutional Convention, 1987–1988

The congressional elections of 1986 derived enormous significance from the imminent plan to transform the Congress into a Constitutional Convention in the following year. The elections ultimately served the interests of the conservatives in this regard: of the 558 members after the elections, only about 10 percent could be regarded as representing leftist parties.[63] The Constitutional Convention consisted of plenary sessions of the Congress, usually held in the mornings; the Congress continued to act as a legislative body at other times.

The emergence of a new, elite-oriented coalition known as the Big Center, which dominated the smaller progressive coalitions, produced a Constitution that was primarily sensitive to elite concerns. A national plan for agrarian reform was rendered inoperative, the military retained its prerogative to intervene in political affairs, and a key provision establishing workers' rights was defeated, although workers' rights were improved to some extent. The defeat of a progressive agrarian reform program that was initially proposed by President-elect Tancredo Neves and strongly embraced after his death by José Sarney was particularly pernicious. The Big Center had effectively lost a unique opportunity in Brazilian history in which a relatively peaceful path to greater economic democracy had been opened.

Progressive provisions were also approved by the Constitutional Convention, although they tended to be unenforceable platitudes. Title II, Chapter I, Article 5, for example, decreed the equality of men and women; outlawed torture; guaranteed freedoms of belief, speech, assembly, access to information; etc. Many provisions seemed specifically aimed at the excesses of dictatorship; e.g., the Constitution declared one's house to be "the inviolable asylum of the individual" and declared that "no one can enter it without the consent of the resident, save for the case of flagrant crime, or disaster, or to render help or, during the day, by judicial determination."[64]

Of key significance in the 1988 Constitution, however, were the strengthening of the National Congress as an institution and the creation of three more rural states by 1990 that would further tip the balance of power in favor of the conservative, machine politics so typical of the past. Enhanced control over the budget[65] was particularly important, although such powers had their potential drawbacks, as the 1993–1994 congressional budget scandal graphically demonstrated. The new Constitution did little to make budgetary information publicly available, and as Barry Ames presciently observes regarding the pre-1964 period in Brazil, "the biggest obstacle to understanding legislative influence in budget-making is the absence of data. Rarely are both legislative budgets and final expenditures available over a period of years, and even more rarely can final expenditures be linked to particular constituencies."[66] The Constitution also provided the basis for powerful new commissions of parliamentary inquiry, which would become critically important in the 1992 impeachment of President Collor and the 1993–1994 congressional scandal.

Perhaps the single most tendentious issue involved the length of the presidential term. With the economy deteriorating and President Sarney's popularity dropping, the progressive coalitions argued for a four-year presidential term. The conservatives, led by Army Minister General Leônidas Pires Gonçalves, insisted upon a five-year term and ultimately won with a vote of 328 to 222 (with three abstentions).[67] As Leonel Brizola, a perennial leftist candidate for the presidency remarked, "Sarney lost three years to gain one more. The weakening of his government will be so great by 1989 that the defeat of his government will be crushing."[68] In retrospect, his comment could have applied equally to the brief respites created by many of the other successful constitutional provisions implemented by the elitists.

The Reluctant Impeachment, 1992

The election in 1989 of a young conservative, Fernando Collor de Mello, to the Brazilian presidency reinforced many of the stereotypes of twentieth-century Brazilian politics. Collor was a member of the elite, had been appointed to his first major political position by the military dictatorship, and had hurriedly put together a weak and amorphous political party for the election. His utter lack of political party support in the Congress, however, was not initially a barrier. For two years he acted with a great deal of congressional support despite his penchant for arbitrary and even bizarre behavior. Moreover, when evidence of his blatantly corrupt and licentious behavior began to emerge, the congressional initiatives to establish an inquiry and move toward impeachment were decidedly sluggish.

The continuing domination of the Congress by political and socioeconomic elites and the dramatic disparity in Brazilian society between the elites and the masses[69] initially suggested the relative unlikelihood of a successful impeachment. Brazil remained a country "whose history is one of continuities rather than ruptures, where pacts among elites, not open conflicts, are the norm."[70] The "democratization," or rather liberalization, process that had ended military dictatorship retained as its central goal the restraint of mass politics.

Luciano Martins characterizes this as a dilemma: "how to 'liberalize' and at the same time block an opposition which proposes immediate distributive and social policies."[71] Presidential impeachment in this context was regarded as a profound political risk to elite politics in Brazil, and hence was approached very reluctantly by Congress.

Collor, however, contributed directly to his own impeachment. He was from the start an extraordinarily vulnerable president in both background and temperament. Given his limited political experience—based upon military appointment and his ascriptive elite status—there is little to indicate that he ever developed basic political judgment. His temperament was even less appropriate to his position. Accounts of his wild parties, his use of illegal drugs, and his meretricious lifestyle both prior to and after assuming the presidency[72] suggest the image of a sybarite rather than that of even a marginally effective politician.

Several factors appear to have been crucial in compelling an otherwise risk-averse and elite-oriented Congress to move to impeach Collor: the blatant character of the alleged corruption; Collor's appeal for mass participation and its unintended consequences; and the format and timing of the inquiry. It is important to recognize the idiosyncratic character of these factors. There does not seem to have been a predetermined progression from one to another. Taken individually, they each were necessary (but not sufficient) conditions of impeachment. As with the Nixon impeachment hearings, to which the Collor crisis was frequently compared,[73] a series of unlikely events had coalesced to compel the Congress to act. P. C. Farias, Collor's infamous campaign fund-raiser, had already been associated with a series of corruption scandals, principal among them the irregularities alleged to have been part of the privatization of the state airline, VASP;[74] the rapid growth of his business empire had also been mentioned repeatedly in the national press. When Collor's brother, Pedro, attacked the corruption of the presidency in a dramatic press conference in May 1992, the key revelation was that Collor knew of the illegal activities of Farias.[75]

As striking ramifications of the numerous kickback schemes gradually became public during the next several months, national attention turned to Collor's luxurious mansion in Brasília, the "Casa de Dinda," which had been renovated at a cost of $2.5 million and featured eight artificial waterfalls and a tropical garden. It was featured in front-page and cover stories for weeks; one story referred to it as the "Garden of the Maharajah of Dinda,"[76] an ironic reference to Collor's campaign against corruption as governor of the state of Alagoas. As the congressional inquiry (initiated in late June) began to trace the sources of funding for the renovation and for cars and other items that the president had acquired, it immediately uncovered a money-laundering scheme, complete with phantom employees and conduits through the Virgin Islands and Panama.[77] Estimates of the extent of the corruption quickly reached into the tens of millions of dollars.[78]

When Collor called on the "silent majority" to come out in support of him by demonstrating in the streets dressed in green and yellow (the national colors) in August 1992, thousands of young people poured into the streets dressed in black in a "war of colors."[79] Brazilian fans at the Olympics in Spain hung banners from the stands calling for Collor's resignation.[80] By September, over 70 percent of the Brazilian population favored his immediate removal, despite the fact that 50 percent held a negative view of Vice-president Itamar Franco,[81] his constitutional successor.

The nature of the congressional inquiry was particularly damaging to Collor. The televised testimony of numerous witnesses, which dominated the airwaves from June through August 1992, was interjected into the most popular prime-time event of the period, the Summer Olympics in Barcelona. The televised inquiry proved to be unexpectedly effective, not only in uncovering a network of money-laundering schemes, but in publicly pressuring specific members of the Congress to support presidential impeachment.

A series of economic and political crises blocked the normal tactics of executive defense that Collor might have used during the last hours before impeachment: a refusal by the finance minister to use federal economic resources to "buy off" the political opposition; the utter erosion of political party support in the Congress for Collor; and the growing impact of mass mobilization on congressional behavior (particularly in the unprecedented demand for a public congressional impeachment vote). This last factor was especially reminiscent of the Diretas Já! campaign. When members of the legislature were held individually accountable for their votes in a popularly explosive and widely televised event, the traditional pattern of elite-oriented converse representation became impossible, and a higher level of democratic representation occurred.

Corruption and the Erosion of Congressional Legitimacy, 1993

The national news magazine *Veja* featured a cover photograph of the congressional budget director on its October 20, 1993, edition. Of considerable interest to the Brazilian public were the handcuffs that he wore. José Carlos Alves dos Santos, arrested for embezzlement, receipt of kickbacks, and murder, soon implicated dozens of members of Congress, many of whom had been widely believed to be above suspicion. Moreover, seven members, dubbed the "seven dwarves" by the media, who were deeply implicated by the allegations began to implicate private companies and colleagues as the scandal widened. The waxing legitimacy of the Congress now turned into a rapid decline.

Coming as it did barely a year after the impeachment of President Collor, the scandal became yet another national political trauma. The military immediately questioned the governability of Brazil. A subsequent revelation that the president of the Chamber of Deputies and leader of the PMDB, Ibsen Pinheiro, was heavily involved in graft was met with the glaring headline "Et tu, Ibsen!"[82] When the governor of the Northeastern state of Paraíba brutally shot a former governor in the face in a restaurant in early November 1993, the crime was attributed to the national turmoil, with one member of Congress remarking that "it is a dangerous situation, and it would not surprise me if similar things came to happen here in the Congress."[83] Subsequent revelations that the nation's major building contractors had engaged in a huge kickback scheme deepened the scandal by year's end.[84]

Brazil has long been typified as an elite-dominated political system that has lacked clear party identity. In a mass democratic structure, some method for attracting mass votes had to be developed. Given Brazil's corporate and authoritarian past, it is not surprising that there has been—and continues to be—a prevalence of political patronage as a vehicle whereby elite politicians with nondescript political party positions can attract mass voters. This widespread patronage and its often kindred spirit, corruption, suggest to some observers "the irresponsible character of much of the Brazilian political class. On the whole, it is a political class known for corruption and clientelism, and it does not always take legislative responsibilities very seriously."[85]

Nevertheless, the congressional commission of inquiry that was established in late 1993 faced a major challenge in 1994: the reestablishment of legitimacy without recourse to another branch of government. The presidency, seriously weakened by Collor's impeachment and the passivity of his replacement, Itamar Franco, has clearly lost the initiative.[86] The military, meanwhile, is cognizant of the enormous national problems—including a persistent monthly inflation rate that exceeds 35 percent and massive unemployment—and is hence unwilling for the time being to return to power. The Congress, it appears, still has a chance to cleanse itself of its corrupt elements and somehow regain a modicum of legitimacy in the year that remains before the next presidential elections. The legislature, for all its blemishes, continues to be an indispensable element in the democratization of Brazil.

Conclusion

The Brazilian National Congress clearly has the power, as established in the 1988 Constitution, to play a key role in the democratization process. Nevertheless, it has never accepted the responsibility to do so; rather, it has repeatedly chosen to act very conservatively and tentatively in broad questions of democracy, while exercising extraordinary (and politically unacceptable) powers in maintaining its own elitist agenda and prerogatives. In the power vacuum that followed the impeachment of President Collor, such individualistic legislative behavior seriously eroded the legitimacy of the Congress and contributed—perhaps irreversibly—to its reputation for individual corruption. As Ronald Schneider concludes, the 1988 Constitution gave the National Congress "broad powers without responsibility for governing, while leaving the president with powers insufficient for his nearly complete responsibility for conducting the nation's governance."[87] With both institutions now reeling from corruption scandals, the prognosis for democratization in Brazil has darkened.

The formative years of the dictatorship, and particularly the four general behavior patterns that came to dominate the legislature at that time (converse representation, opposition posturing, limited crisis management, and passive acquiescence to overt cooptation), seem to have established a "legislative culture" that has remained a dominant influence in the Brazilian Congress. Of decidedly secondary importance, unfortunately, have been the needs and potential of the people of Brazil.

The development of legislative politics during the past two decades does include unquestionably democratic aspects. For example, the Congress has fully explored a range of tactics in opposing arbitrary executive authority. In the context of Brazilian history, effective opposition to the executive is, ceteris paribus, democratization. Moreover, the legislature has increasingly learned to respond to mass popular pressures and has thus become far more representative of its national constituency than ever before. The congressional corruption scandal might even be regarded with a modicum of pride as evidence of the beginning of a new political order in Brazil.

Nevertheless, in an era of relentless inflation, economic dysfunction, social violence, and public humiliation of the presidency, the antidemocratic implications of the diminishing legitimacy of a scandal-plagued Congress are all too clear. General Benedito Onofre Leonel, chief of the general staff of the army, at a commissioning of military officers on December 9, 1993, is reported to have quoted the ancient Roman officer Marcus Flavius: "They tell me that in Rome intrigues and conspiracies succeed, treason develops, and many, hesitant, perturbed, easily give in to the worst temptations of abandon and degrade our nation." Leonel emphasized Flavius's conclusion: "Beware the wrath of the legions."[88]

Postscript

The impressive first-round election victory of Fernando Henrique Cardoso to the presidency in October, 1994 (with 54 percent of the vote) followed a dramatic drop in inflation after the introduction of a new currency, the Real. The October congressional elections, however, seem to have perpetuated legislative intransigence. The party coalition that supported Cardoso—his PSDB (Party of Brazilian Social Democracy), along with the PFL (Liberal Front Party), PTB (Brazilian Labor Party) and PL (Liberal Party)—are far from holding a majority. Furthermore, a combination of widespread urban crime, white-collar corruption and threats of renewed inflation will inevitably force Cardoso to confront the Congress. With its sixteen different political parties, and its unique institutional history and functions, it remains a deeply divided legislature. Plus ça change . . .

Notes

The author would like to thank the University of Idaho Research Council and the Martin Institute for Peace Studies and Conflict Resolution (University of Idaho) for research grants that facilitated field research in Brazil. An earlier version of this chapter was presented at the Seventeenth International Congress of the Latin American Studies Association in Los Angeles on September 25, 1992. The author would like to thank Martin C. Needler, David Close, Barry Ames, and Timothy Power for their helpful comments.

1. See, e.g., Alfred Stepan, *The Military in Politics: Changing Patterns in Brazil* (Princeton, New Jersey: Princeton University Press, 1971); Stepan, *The State and Society: Peru in Comparative Perspective* (Princeton, New Jersey: Princeton University Press, 1978); David Collier (ed.), *The New Authoritarianism in Latin America* (Princeton, New Jersey: Princeton University Press, 1979).

2. Samuel P. Huntington, *The Third Wave: Democratization in the Late Twentieth Century* (Norman, Oklahoma: University of Oklahoma Press, 1991).

3. Several recent works examine the PT because of its anomalous char-

acter in the Brazilian context, and hence its potential for influencing systemic change. See, for example, Margaret E. Keck, *The Workers' Party and Democratization in Brazil* (New Haven and London: Yale University Press, 1992); Francisco Weffort (ed.), *PT: Um Projeto para o Brasil* (São Paulo: Editora Brasiliense, 1989); Emir Sader and Ken Silverstein, *Without Fear of Being Happy: Lula, the Workers Party and Brazil* (London and New York: Verso, 1991).

4. Robert H. Dix notes in this regard that "although it seems that strong parties are not necessary for inaugurating democratic regimes (although they might be helpful in doing so), they are almost certainly necessary for the long-term consolidation of broad-based representative government." Dix, "Democratization and the Institutionalization of Latin American Political Parties," *Comparative Political Studies*, Vol. 24, No. 4 (January 1992), p. 489.

5. Stepan, *The Military in Politics*, pp. 74–75.

6. Riordan Roett, *Brazil: Politics in a Patrimonial Society* (Boston: Allyn and Bacon, 1972), p. 176.

7. Alfred Stepan notes that during the nadir of the twenty-one-year military dictatorship, "Congress [became] an important index of the proregime civilians in Brazil's federal system, since it [was] here that many of the most powerful groups within the political system publicly articulate[d] their demands." Stepan, *The Military in Politics*, p. 74. It was during this period, according to Thomas Skidmore, that the Congress itself (as an institution) could best be described as "a compliant façade of a Congress, shorn of any independent powers." Skidmore, "Politics and Economic Policy Making in Authoritarian Brazil, 1937–71," in *Authoritarian Brazil: Origins, Policies, and Future*, ed. by Alfred Stepan (New Haven and London: Yale University Press, 1973), p. 16.

8. Scott Mainwaring, "Brazilian Party Underdevelopment in Comparative Perspective," *Political Science Quarterly*, Vol. 107, No. 4 (1992–93), p. 685.

9. Ibid., p. 702.

10. Ibid., p. 705.

11. Ibid., pp. 698–699. He notes that "presidents have perceived parties as obstacles to realizing their objectives rather than agents for helping to achieve them. Their actions against parties and their efforts to construct a political system in which parties are not key actors have contributed to the secular weakness of parties."

12. The impeachment of President Fernando Collor de Mello in 1992 affected this, although the massive congressional budget scandal of 1993–1994 has determined that Congress would not necessarily gain power from the executive's loss.

13. There are several key exceptions to this, e.g., the excellent work of Professors Barry Ames (Washington University, St. Louis), Timothy Power (Louisiana State University), and Abdo I. Baaklini (SUNY-Albany) in the United States; and Vamireh Chacon, David Fleischer, Francisco Weffort, and Bolívar Lamounier in Brazil.

14. This refers to a "Belgium" within an "India," suggesting that a population with about the size and socioeconomic status of Belgium is nested within a much larger population that lives at (or even below) the level of most South Asians.

15. Levy, "Mexico: Sustained Civilian Rule Without Democracy," *Democracy in Developing Countries: Latin America*, Vol. 4, ed. by Larry Diamond, Juan J. Linz, and Seymour Martin Lipset (Boulder, Colorado: Lynne Rienner, 1989), p. 463.

16. José Alvaro Moisés, "Elections, Political Parties and Political Culture in Brazil: Changes and Continuities," *Journal of Latin American Studies,* Vol. 25 (1993), p. 576.

17. Abdo I. Baaklini, *The Brazilian Legislature and Political System* (Westport, Connecticut: Greenwood Press, 1992), p. 24.

18. Peter McDonough, *Power and Ideology in Brazil* (Princeton, New Jersey: Princeton University Press, 1981), p. 198.

19. Douglas A. Chalmers, "Dilemmas of Latin American Democratization: Dealing with International Forces," *Papers on Latin America,* No. 18 (New York: Columbia University, The Institute of Latin American and Iberian Studies, 1990), p. 5.

20. Although, as Bolívar Lamounier notes, as early as the nineteenth century an elitist "parliamentary monarchy" had emerged in which, because of the lack of a threat to the civilian elite, "cabinets were elected and governed, liberals and conservatives rotated in office, and representative practices thus developed to some extent." Lamounier, "Brazil: Inequality Against Democracy," *Democracy in Developing Countries: Latin America,* Vol. 4, ed. by Larry Diamond, Juan J. Linz, and Seymour Martin Lipset (Boulder, Colorado: Lynne Rienner, 1989), p. 117.

21. Skidmore, "Politics and Economic Policy Making," p. 28.

22. There is an abundant literature on this. An especially clear account is Gláucio Ary Dillon Soares, "Military Authoritarianism and Executive Absolutism in Brazil," *Studies in Comparative International Development,* Vol. 14, Nos. 3/4 (Fall/Winter 1979), pp. 104–126. Soares mentions several key military policies that immediately undercut legislative power, including the prohibition of legislative amendments (or changes) to executive bills, the institution of strict deadlines for the ratification of executive proposals, the prohibition of congressional legislation that changed the structure of the military, a vast increase in the number of bills introduced by the executive, and the summary termination in 1969 of parliamentary immunity. One result of these early policies of the dictatorship was a major increase in the rejection by Congress of bills that originated with the legislature, what Soares calls "a kind of legislative suicide" [p. 117].

23. Levy, "Mexico," p. 489. This fits a historical pattern in Brazil, as Richard Graham observes: "In retrospect the historian may be tempted to think of Brazilian elites as paranoid in their constant fear of disorder—since, in fact, no revolution occurred. But this nonoccurrence may be seen, rather, as a great tribute to their skill at combining persuasion with force. For a constant movement of people, a repeated questioning of the individual's place, and a steady tremor of minor protest against violations of the paternalistic code regularly jarred Brazilian social and political life." *Patronage and Politics in Nineteenth-Century Brazil* (Stanford, California: Stanford University Press, 1990), pp. 269–270.

24. Philippe Faucher, "The Paradise That Never Was: The Breakdown of the Brazilian Authoritarian Order," *Authoritarian Capitalism: Brazil's Contemporary Economic and Political Development,* ed. by Thomas C. Bruneau and Philippe Faucher (Boulder, Colorado: Westview Press, 1981), p. 32.

25. Bolívar Lamounier notes in this regard that "the views that do operate in the political system (i.e., those put forward by influential writers, journalists, and the like) show a pervasive and persistent concern, indeed an obsession, with the alleged incongruence between elite and mass culture. Since the early decades of this century, outstanding writers of different persuasions have insisted that powerful cultural strains tend to undermine the idea of a

Western-style democracy in Brazil." Lamounier, "Brazil: Inequality Against Democracy," p. 141.

26. Schmitter found that only 8 percent of interest association leaders saw the Congress as a focus of primary lobbying interest. *Interest Conflict and Political Change in Brazil* (Stanford, California: Stanford University Press, 1971), p. 261. Furthermore, the only two groups that were consistent lobbyists in the legislature, government employees and representatives of cities/counties (*municipalistas*), were groups "whose interests directly coincide[d] with those of the professional politicians in the Congress" [p. 270].

27. Schmitter, *Interest Conflict*, p. 264.

28. Soares, "Military Authoritarianism," p. 120.

29. Thomas E. Skidmore, *The Politics of Military Rule in Brazil, 1864–85* (New York: Oxford University Press, 1988), p. 172.

30. As Skidmore succinctly concludes, "Brazilian authoritarianism had rendered both the non-elite and elite institutions of civil society incapable of significant autonomous action." Skidmore, *The Politics of Military Rule*, p. 181.

31. *Veja*, October 14, 1987, p. 39.

32. Elio Gaspari, "As Vivandeiras do PT," *Veja*, December 8, 1993, p. 47.

33. Skidmore, *The Politics of Military Rule*, p. 27.

34. Peter Flynn, *Brazil: A Political Analysis* (Boulder, Colorado: Westview Press, 1978), p. 325.

35. Thomas E. Skidmore, *Politics in Brazil, 1930–1964; An Experiment in Democracy* (New York: Oxford University Press, 1967), p. 308.

36. Maria Helena Moreira Alves, *State and Opposition in Military Brazil* (Austin: University of Texas Press, 1985), p. 34.

37. Skidmore, *The Politics of Military Rule*, p. 20.

38. Skidmore, "Politics and Economic Policy Making," p. 14.

39. Barry Ames, *Political Survival: Politicians and Public Policy in Latin America* (Berkeley: University of California Press, 1987), p. 145.

40. Robert R. Kaufman, "Liberalization and Democratization in South America: Perspectives from the 1970s," in *Transitions from Authoritarian Rule: Comparative Perspectives*, ed. by Guillermo O'Donnell, Philippe Schmitter, and Laurence Whitehead (Baltimore: Johns Hopkins University Press, 1986), p. 95.

41. Amaury de Souza, "O Sistema Político-Partidário," in *Sociedade, Estado e Partidos na Atualidade Brasileira*, ed. by Helio Jaguaribe (Rio de Janeiro: Paz e Terra, 1992), p. 164.

42. Baaklini, *The Brazilian Legislature*, pp. 39–40.

43. Ibid., p. 25.

44. Skidmore, "Politics and Economic Policy Making," pp. 43–44.

45. Ibid., p. 16.

46. Robert Packenham, "Legislatures and Political Development," in *Legislatures in Developmental Perspective*, ed. by Allan Kornberg and Lloyd Musolf (Durham, North Carolina: Duke University Press, 1970), pp. 529–532.

47. Abdo Baaklini notes that "the measures introduced by the regime to weaken the Congress were not without supporters within the Congress." *The Brazilian Legislature*, p. 49.

48. Schmitter notes that before the coup, nearly two-thirds of the projects approved by the Congress originated from within that body. "By 1971 this had fallen to 27 percent and virtually 100 percent of the proposals 'suggested' to the legislature by the executive were approved." "The 'Portugalization' of Brazil?" in *Authoritarian Brazil*, ed. by Alfred Stepan, pp. 222–223.

49. Daniel Zirker, "Civilianization and Authoritarian Nationalism in Brazil: Ideological Opposition Within a Military Dictatorship," *Journal of Political and Military Sociology*, Vol. 14, No. 2 (Fall 1986), pp. 263–276. A similar fractionalization among the military was evident at the end of the Greek military dictatorship. Constantine Danopoulos, "From Balconies to Tanks: Post Junta Civil-Military Relations in Greece," *Journal of Political and Military Sociology*, Vol. 13, No. 1 (Spring 1985), pp. 83–98.

50. A visit to Brazil in 1972 by the U.S. political scientist Samuel P. Huntington resulted in a 1973 invited paper entitled "Approaches to Political Decompression," in which Huntington warns against uncontrolled liberalization and recommends the Mexican political party model as an effective solution. By 1974, Huntington had returned to Brazil to give a seminar entitled "Legislatures and Development." Skidmore, *The Politics of Military Rule*, pp. 165, 170.

51. Skidmore, *The Politics of Military Rule*, p. 191.

52. As Barry Ames puts it, "that these [liberalizing] stratagems failed rather ignominiously in no way detracts from their importance as survival tactics." *Political Survival*, p. 227.

53. Baaklini, *The Brazilian Legislature*, p. 41.

54. Ronald M. Schneider, *"Order and Progress": A Political History of Brazil* (Boulder, Colorado: Westview Press, 1991), p. 282.

55. Bolívar Lamounier (interview), *Veja*, December 29, 1993, p. 8.

56. Schneider, *"Order and Progress,"* pp. 290–291.

57. Skidmore, *The Politics of Military Rule*, p. 241.

58. The new Workers' Party was an exception to this rule.

59. Skidmore, *The Politics of Military Rule*, pp. 241–243.

60. The widely unpopular Paulo Maluf had received the nomination of the government party, and this gave the PMDB the possibility of winning the election in the electoral college with their candidate, Tancredo Neves. Military threats from hard-line general Newton Cruz during the Diretas Já! campaign likely influenced the outcome of the congressional vote as well. *Veja*, May 2, 1984, pp. 32–34.

61. Alfred Stepan, *Rethinking Military Politics; Brazil and the Southern Cone* (Princeton, New Jersey: Princeton University Press, 1988), p. 61.

62. *Veja*, September 12, 1984, p. 28.

63. Baaklini, *The Brazilian Legislature*, p. 161.

64. *Constituição da República Federativa do Brasil, 1988* (Brasília: Editora Tecnoprint, 1988), pp. 9–10.

65. Baaklini, *The Brazilian Legislature*, p. 191.

66. Ames, "The Congressional Connection, the Structure of Politics, and the Distribution of Public Expenditures in Brazil's Competitive Period," *Comparative Politics*, No. 19 (1987), pp. 147–148.

67. Five members of the 1986 Congress had died by this time.

68. Quoted in *Veja*, June 8, 1988, p. 36.

69. This dualism, which leads to the characterization of the country as "Belindia," is well documented in Helio Jaguaribe, et al., *Brasil: Reforma ou Caos*, 6th edition (Rio de Janeiro: Editora Paz e Terra, 1991), p. 17 ff. Jacques Lambert calls it the "two Brazils." *Os Dois Brasís* (Rio de Janeiro: Centro Brasileiro de Pesquisas Educacionais, 1959).

70. Emir Sader and Ken Silverstein, *Without Fear of Being Happy*, p. 17.

71. Luciano Martins, "The 'Liberalization' of Authoritarian Rule in Brazil," in *Transitions from Authoritarian Rule: Latin America*, ed. by Guillermo

O'Donnell, Philippe Schmitter, and Laurence Whitehead (Baltimore: The Johns Hopkins University Press, 1986), p. 80.

72. *Veja,* in a cover story entitled "Sex, Drugs and Fights in Dinda [Collor's house]," describes Collor's bisexuality and drugged licentiousness at great length, concluding that "if one-tenth of what is known today about the past of Fernando Collor had been known in 1989, it would have been difficult for him to be elected. Brazil would not have passed through two years of ruin and thievery." March 17, 1993, p. 21.

73. See, for example, Raymundo Faoro, "Um Adendo ao Impeachment," *Istoé,* July 15, 1992, p. 25.

74. *Veja,* July 3, 1991. The article describes P. C. Farias as the "greatest symbol of the group of the Republic of Alagoas [a Brazilian state], and noted that upon his recent return from the United States, his baggage was not inspected despite the obvious presence of expensive purchases" [pp. 20–21].

75. Collor's brother announced to the media, "I do not believe that he [the president] knew of all of the cases, all of the methods, all of the attributes of Paulo [Farias] in relation to A, B, C, or D. But that he knew that Paulo acted in his name, I did know. Paulo said '70 percent is for the boss and 30 percent is mine.' . . . The president perhaps did not know of all of the forms, all of the areas, all of the sources that Paulo touched, but he knew that Paulo acted in his name." *Veja,* May 27, 1992, p. 24.

76. *Veja,* September 9, 1992.

77. *Istoé,* August 25, 1992, p. 24.

78. Estimates of $52 million are regarded as "modest." *Veja,* March 17, 1993, p. 17.

79. *Latin American Weekly Report,* August 27, 1992, p. 1.

80. *Istoé,* August 5, 1992, p. 11.

81. *Latin American Weekly Report,* October 8, 1992, p. 1.

82. "Até Tu, Ibsen," *Veja,* November 17, 1993, cover.

83. A quote from Mário Covas, *Veja,* November 10, 1993, p. 34.

84. *Latin American Weekly Report,* November 11, 1993, p. 518. The chair of the legislative commission of inquiry investigating the congressional corruption scandal, Senator Jarbas Passarinho (a retired army colonel), referred to the massive Italian corruption investigation and concluded that "if we do not repeat what has been done in Italy it will be very difficult for the population to believe in democracy." *Latin American Weekly Report—Brazil Report,* November 25, 1993, p. 1.

85. Mainwaring, "Brazilian Party Underdevelopment," p. 696. He continues: "Clientelism has a legitimate place in politics, but in Brazil clientelistic activities have predominated at the expense of legislative functions. Even in the constitutional congress [1987–1988], major issues were often debated in cavalier fashion. Many politicians had a poor grasp of the issues, and the quality of debates was usually dismal."

86. As Bolívar Lamounier puts it, Itamar "threw extraordinary political capital out the window. In the moment that he assumed power, if he had shown more affirmative leadership, [appointed] a moral cabinet, and [adopted] a more defined line of behavior, we would have gained time and economized suffering." *Veja,* December 29, 1993, p. 9.

87. Schneider, *"Order and Progress,"* p. 384.

88. Quoted in *Veja,* December 15, 1993, p. 38.

6

Legislatures and Democratic Transitions in Latin America: The Chilean Case

Jorge Nef and Nibaldo Galleguillos

The purpose of this essay is to analyze the role of Chilean parliamentary institutions and practices in the country's democratic development. We have intentionally concentrated on recent history, rather than on the abundant pre-1973 literature. Among Latin American nations Chile possessed a long and honorable tradition of parliamentary rule, including a parliamentary republic between 1891 and 1924. In the 1960s, it was reputedly among the top countries in the world, considered to be stable, democratic, and politically developed. Yet tradition was no safeguard against the emergence of one of the world's most repressive dictatorships scarcely a decade later: Chilean democracy came to a sudden end in the bloody military coup that overthrew the Allende presidency and simultaneously destroyed the pluralistic and parliamentary trappings of the old republic. It is our contention that "classical" Chilean democracy is less relevant to understanding the present than it is to explaining the republic's rupture and the emergence of the dictatorial regime. In this sense, although not discounting elements of institutional continuity, the system of government that emerged in 1990 after the orderly retreat of the long-lasting military dictatorship is rooted more in Chile's recent antidemocratic origins than in its remote democratic past.

We believe that a better, more concrete, and noncircular answer to the question of what the contribution of parliamentary politics is to the strengthening of liberal democracy can be given by concentrating on postcoup developments. We suggest that the much-hailed "redemocratization" and the role of parliamentary politics in both phases of such democratization—transition and consolidation—must be seen in the light of three specific and more recent developments. One such development concerns the *processes* of transition that enabled the current Congress to come into existence. The second is the development of the *mechanisms for producing officials* that led to the actual configuration of Congress, including how candidates were nominated, whose sectors they came to represent, and the system of coalition building prior to the aforementioned election. The third development involves the actual *consequences of the democratizing initiatives* undertaken jointly by Congress and the executive during the 1990–1993 legislative period, which coincides with the four-year tenure of President Patricio Aylwin, a Christian Democrat.

The Transition to Democracy

To begin with, the nature of the process of transition from the authoritarian military regime that ruled the country for sixteen years to the democratically elected civilian government needs to be unraveled. This lengthy process was characterized by shifting offensive-defensive phases adopted, according to political conjunctures, by the ruling civilian-military coalition. It was also a multifaceted counterrevolutionary process that attempted to eradicate and overhaul the ways in which Chileans used to conduct their political affairs. Above all, while modernizing Chile's capitalist model of accumulation, the Pinochet regime aimed at preventing the type of political stalemate that characterized Chilean politics in the years before the military takeover. This involved a sustained effort at keeping popular mobilization to a minimum. In other words, to understand the nature of the transition *to* bureaucratic authoritarianism, one must gain an insight into the profound socioeconomic and political cleavages that underpinned the Chilean state. Conversely, an analysis of the transition *from* bureaucratic authoritarianism needs to start precisely with an analysis of the dynamics of the military regime. In particular, we must emphasize those aspects of the latter transition geared to limiting the potentially democratizing role of the emerging legislative body while consolidating a new political order that in its essence was to be profoundly undemocratic.

The Authoritarian "Software"

The transition was carefully shaped and guided by the "reactionary coalition" that effectively ruled the country from September 1973 to March 1990. The main goal of this coalition was to entrench and institutionalize a restrictive political regime based upon an elitist class alliance and committed to consolidating an extreme form of the neoliberal socioeconomic model. The ideological basis of the corresponding institutional order was an extremely militaristic and corporatist interpretation of the so-called National Security Doctrine (NSD). In General Augusto Pinochet's own words: "The State assumes with determination a clear, firm, and vigorous doctrine—that of national security. From that doctrine emanates the juridical basis of the new Chilean institutional order that is indissoluble from the very State."[1]

This, in turn, translated into copious de facto legislation defining the juridical software of a political "game" clearly at odds with both Chile's past democratic traditions and established Western democratic practices elsewhere. The "algorithmic" NSD package included, among other things, the 1976 Constitutional Acts 2, 3, and 4; the 1980 Constitution; the 1989 Anti-Terrorist Law; the 1989 Electoral Laws; and the 1989 constitutional amendments. All of these concentrated power in an all-powerful executive: General Pinochet, who was also the head of the military establishment. The legislation (inspired by the regime's main corporatist thinker, Jaime Guzmán) reflected a negative view of liberal democracy, which the regime rejected outright.[2] General Pinochet solemnly declared in a 1977 speech that the new democracy was to be

> *authoritarian,* insofar as it must be provided with a strong and vigorous authority and be capable of enforcing a juridical system that truly guarantees the rights of the people, under the adequate protection of independent courts of law invested with sufficient authority to obtain observance of its resolutions; *protected,* insofar as it must guarantee the fundamental concept of our Declaration of Principles as a basic doctrine of the State of Chile, thereby replacing the classical, candid, and defenseless liberal state by a new one committed to freedom and the dignity of man and the essential values of our nationhood. Consequently, any assault on these principles, the content of which has been gradually established by the Constitutional Acts currently in effect, is considered to represent an illicit act against the institutional order of the Republic. Freedom and democracy cannot survive if they are deprived of the means required to defend themselves against those who seek to destroy them; *integrating,* insofar as it must strengthen the National Objectives and Permanent Objectives of the Nation, in order that beyond all legitimate differences in other more circumstantial aspects, coming governments may reflect in the future the essential continuity that they have been lacking in the past. This will create a powerful element of unity among the great Chilean family, for so long the target of systematic attempts to disunite it by promoting a struggle of classes that does not and never should exist; *technical,* insofar as the whirling scientific and technological progress of the world today cannot be ignored. . . . This alone will enable us to place discussion at an adequate degree and level, to reduce the

margin of ideological debate to its true proportions and thus take advantage of the contributions provided by the most capable; with *authentic social participation,* insofar as a society is truly and fully free only to the extent that, on the basis of the principle of subsidiarity, it consecrates and respects the real autonomy of intermediate groups between the individual and the State, in pursuing their own and specific purposes. This principle is the basis for a social body gifted with creative vitality, as well as for economic freedom that, in observance of the rules established by the State authorities in protection of the common good, will prevent individuals from suffocating under the yoke of an almighty State.[3]

The aforementioned "authentic social participation" was unequivocally a form of "functional" representation by social forces: corporatism. The regime's obvious mistrust of political competition, political parties, and parliamentary politics as a whole was matched only by its instrumental belief that autonomous intermediate groups—communities, *gremios,* and corporations—are the best mechanisms for societal integration. For instance, Article 1.3 of the Constitution states: "The State recognizes and protects the intermediate groups through which society is organized and structured; it guarantees them the necessary autonomy in the accomplishment of their specific goals." This disposition ratifies Article 5 of Institutional Act 2, which says that "Chile is a republic that is being instituted as a new democracy with community participation and provided with the tools required to guarantee its protection, strength, and authority." Thus, the constitutional clause declaring that sovereignty resides in the nation—not the people—became the formalization of a deeply rooted antidemocratic belief.

Systemic Exclusion

The legal-institutional order sought by the ruling coalition had a strong bias against any sort of popular input or citizen participation. The above-mentioned legislation was seldom discussed in public fora. Debates on the form and substance of the new polity were restricted to a handful of individuals within the inner clique. It was a new "social contract" but without transparency, a real presence, or consent of the sectors most affected by it. Participation by most Chileans was limited to their being asked to ratify the 1980 Constitution in a highly fraudulent referendum that, not surprisingly, gave the dictatorship a decisive majority. The new political regime also included a vigorous condemnation of the country's traditional political party system and pluralistic brokerage, a feature that had set Chile apart from its Latin American counterparts. In blaming political parties for the country's

ills, General Pinochet, a mouthpiece for traditional Chilean undemocratic sectors, stated:

> One of the most serious crises of contemporary democracy could be
> found in that, under the protection of inadequate constitutional sys-
> tems, political parties have become mere vehicles through which to
> reach power and wherein a small group of leaders, devoid of any title
> or legal responsibility whatsoever, belittle and condition popular par-
> ticipation. . . . The new institutional system demands the design of a
> juridical scheme that clearly establishes that in it there would and
> could not be any room for the traditional political parties, inasmuch
> as their structure, leaders, habits, and mentality had been framed
> under the inspiration of a constitutional system that has definitely
> ceased to exist. The intention is to clear the way to depart in the
> future from the concept of the old political parties, which so greatly
> facilitated the predominance of demagoguery and Marxist infiltra-
> tion, to a conception of political parties under which they merely rep-
> resent flows of opinion. This conception involves abandoning the
> idea that political parties are corporate bodies under public law that,
> supported by election procedures that enable them a practical
> monopoly on citizen vote and political participation, become vast
> power-holding machineries, often financed by foreign or interna-
> tional organizations, the interests of which they invariably end up
> serving.[4]

The drafters of the Constitution also assured themselves that, in
the event that groups or individuals espousing views contrary to the
counterrevolution got elected to Congress, mechanisms should be in
place that could handcuff them in terms of what they could accomplish there. Accordingly, the Constitution severely sanctioned those
members of Congress who would take sides in labor, student, or other
social disputes.[5] Likewise, representatives from the popular sectors are
also constrained from running for office by virtue of some constitutional clauses that forbid trade union leaders from belonging to political parties. In addition, the requisite that candidates must have completed their high-school education played against the representatives
of the popular sectors. The first limitation places a heavy economic
burden on those aspiring to run for public office because they cannot
count on the financial support provided by a party; the second limitation guarantees that only the relatively well-educated sectors can participate in competitive politics.

Antiparliamentary Biases

As the new institutional order was being built, the Pinochet regime
came to accept that a legislature was a necessary evil that the "future
democracy" could not do without, especially if the drafters of the

Constitution wished Chile to be counted within the "Free World" camp. What they could do, however, as their Brazilian counterparts had done after 1964, was wrest away many of the attributes traditionally granted to Congress. Thus, the policymaking functions of the future legislature were made extremely limited, especially when compared with those enjoyed before the 1973 military coup. Formerly a proactive, engaging, and dynamic institution, Congress was now to be transformed into a paper tiger.[6]

The nature of executive-legislative relations was itself to be altered in such way that the traditional balance between these two institutions was now to be tilted toward the former. However, the antecedents of the situation since 1989 were established during the early years of the military dictatorship. In effect, during this period the role of the legislature was assumed by the government junta. Decree-Law 527 (June 26, 1974) stated that "the decision to legislate is the exclusive prerogative of the government junta" (Article 5). However, Article 8 came to qualify those attributes by stating that "members of the government junta will cooperate with its president in the exercise of the executive functions that fall within his power, by accepting his orders with respect to the activities, jurisdictions, and functions assigned by the president."[7] The new political system became, at least on the surface, one of unrestricted presidentialism. Most matters of importance remain the privilege of the president, as indicated in Articles 62 and 64 of the Constitution.[8]

Accordingly, among the fewer prerogatives granted to elected congresspersons were that the Chamber of Deputies could oversee the executive's actions but that its resolutions or observations could not affect the political responsibilities of cabinet ministers (Article 48.1). The only requirement for the executive was simply to give an answer to the Chamber of Deputies. The severely handicapped Chamber of Deputies is the only place where bills concerning taxation, public services' budget, and matters dealing with the military draft can first be discussed. Yet, in these affairs the executive always has the upper hand and the almost exclusive initiative. The same is true regarding the relationships between the executive and the Senate. The Senate is where first discussion of bills granting amnesty or general indults takes place (Article 62).[9] These matters are also ones of exclusive presidential initiative.

The Power Map

Real political power was effectively to reside in a number of unelected, unrepresentative, undemocratic, and unaccountable institutions whose main function was to defend the counterrevolutionary order from the vagaries of political competition. Prominent among them were two self-generating organizations possessing "metapower": the armed forces and the judiciary.[10] These two entities extend their fiscalizing jurisdiction onto the nation's politics, economics, and security: they are entitled by the Constitution to appoint some of their own to the Senate, the national security council, the constitutional tribunal, the national electoral tribunal, and the lower electoral courts. One of the most remarkable features of the new institutional order is that the armed forces and the judiciary have seen their attributes and prerogatives strengthened by the Constitution. The irony here cannot be missed: these are the same entities whose inspired defense of the country's democratic traditions before September 11, 1973, proved to be purely formal. Acting in unison, they complemented each other in dismantling the previous democratic regime. The brutality of the military was matched only by the willingness of the judiciary to ignore, if not legitimize, the abrogation of civil and political rights after the fateful coup.

In addition, the drafters of the Constitution proceeded to legislate what amounted to a "dictatorship of the minority." In effect, they stipulated that in order to reform the Constitution a two-thirds majority must be attained.[11] Such difficult-to-reach quorums make it easy for the supporters of the authoritarian institutional order to block constitutional reforms initiatives, particularly those aimed at democratizing the country.

Fail-safe Mechanisms and Overriding Commands

Finally, in order to ensure the permanence over time of the newly created economic, social, and political system, the 1980 Constitution granted the armed forces the role of a "reserve power." When everything else fails, the ruling sectors can still count on the military to come to "the defense of the fatherland, national security, and the institutional order of the republic."[12] Put simply, what this disposition states is that the same social sectors who created the new institutional order are also responsible for its preservation. Again, notions of popular sovereignty or the natural right of rebellion, which the civilian-military coalition constantly used in order to justify the 1973 coup, are but a cloak with which to hide the elitist nature of the new regime.

It must be stressed that the above-described constitutional matrix and political institutions constituted the devices imposed on the opposition to the military regime to "guide" and effect the "transition to democracy." That is, the rules, the agenda, and the final arbitrators granted the ability to control outcomes by altering the rules of the game to those sectors theoretically defeated in the 1988 plebiscite. The democratic opposition had no choice but to abide by these "rules of the game." We must understand, however, that the pre-1990 regime was not just a suprastructural repressive system. The socioeconomic result of the long period of military rule was, as already mentioned, a thorough counterrevolution that succeeded in restructuring and modernizing the foundations of Chilean capitalism while drastically weakening popular organizations. Liberal capitalism had been replaced by authoritarian—or "illiberal"—capitalism.

Thus, the transition away from authoritarianism was characterized by an extremely uneven power balance. On the one hand there was a much smaller, disorganized, and fragmented labor movement, loosely aligned with a powerless, shrinking, and highly depoliticized middle class. On the other, there was a highly integrated, articulated, and powerful business class, structurally allied with a seemingly omnipotent military establishment and strongly supported by business and military constituencies abroad.

The Genesis of the New Parliament: The 1989 General Election

The completion of the transition from the bureaucratic authoritarian regime toward a "protected" democracy was to be a "function of the degree of maturity" displayed by Chilean society.[13] According to the dictatorship and its supporters, such maturity was not to be reached before 1991. In the meantime, Chileans were expected to place themselves under the guiding hand of an absolute ruler: General Pinochet. In effect, the 1980 Constitution extended his mandate until 1988, when limited political participation was to be granted. At that time, Chileans could expect to participate in a plebiscite in order to ratify the "new president" proposed by the military junta. The new president was expected to be, again, General Pinochet, to whom explicit regulations forbidding reelection would not apply.

This well-planned "transition to nowhere," however, turned into one of the greatest blunders to be made by the dictatorship. Despite the oft-repeated "success" of the economic model and in spite of fragmentation, fear, and propaganda, once asked to choose, the electorate responded with a strong rejection of Pinochet's "New Republic." The general, to his amazement, was soundly defeated.[14] In effect, presented with their first real opportunity to pass judgment on fifteen years of dictatorship, most Chileans did not hesitate to show their contempt for authoritarian and undemocratic politics.

Although the regime's first reaction was to backtrack on its promises to lead the transition to fruitful completion, this option was not possible, in part because of international public opinion pressure (including that of its closest ally, the United States) and also because of a swell of internal political mobilization. The opposition had brought together a cross section of Chilean society that became active in demanding that the military government play the political game in accordance to the rules that it had designed. Thus, the regime had little choice but to move ahead with the scheduled transition. This meant calling a real general election to select both a new president and a new parliament on December 14, 1989. However, the regime's decision to play according to its own rules signaled that the 1980 Constitution, with all its restrictive stipulations, was now to become fully operational.

The months leading to the December election were full of ebullient optimism on the part of the opposition forces, who anticipated a victory for Patricio Aylwin, a Christian Democrat. A similar outcome was less likely for the proregime forces, who early on in the campaign trail threw in the towel with regard to winning the presidential election. The real competition then became one for the seats in the new legislature. Both the regime supporters (now clustered in a coalition known as Democracy and Progress) and its opponents (grouped in the Agreement for Democracy coalition) realized that the dismantling of the institutional order created by the civilian-military regime could be accomplished only by means of a significant majority control of Congress. According to the rules carefully engineered by the military regime, this realization meant that the first coalition could not afford to lose by too wide a margin; Democracy and Progress needed to obtain a sufficient minority capable of blocking the new government's attempts to democratize the Chilean political process. For the democratic opposition, however, "victory" required a landslide to provide the quorums needed to transform the authoritarian order into a more democratic one, legally, constitutionally, and (most important) peacefully.

Thus, a rush for control of the new parliament got under way. However, the entire process surrounding the forthcoming elections was not going to take place in accordance with traditional liberal democratic practices. Rather, it was to be in accordance with the rules created by the authoritarian regime, which the opposition forces had chosen to abide by. Moreover, because politics of an open and competitive sort had been suspended for so long, there was a sense of urgency in mobilizing former and new supporters among the political parties that were just beginning to resurface. Grassroots participation was deemed expendable for the time being in the new context of a "pact of elites." The nomination of candidates remained the preserve of appointments made by a handful of moderate "notables" who, for a variety of reasons, had made a name for themselves during the dictatorship. Those nominated represented a very small segment of Chilean society, namely the middle, upper-middle, and upper classes.[15]

Almost completely shut out of this first democratic exercise were the representatives of the popular movement against the dictatorship: human rights organizations, labor, peasants, the urban poor, women, native communities, traditional Marxist and leftist political parties, and the significant Chilean diaspora. The skewness of this situation is even more startling when one recalls that it was precisely these excluded sectors who, beginning in 1983, spearheaded the opposition against the dictatorship, when many notables ran for cover. It is the resilience of the popular movement in resisting governmental repression that better explains the failure of the dictatorship to gain national—and also international—legitimacy. In sum, the "people," as José Nun suggests in his discussions on democratic transition, have come to perform the role that the chorus performs in Greek plays: they appear when needed but are sent backstage when the principal characters in the tragedy return to play the main roles.[16] That is, the populace appear as purely instrumental pawns in a much larger chess game beyond their control.

In spite of the relatively elitist social homogeneity found among those competing for public office, the military regime still showed a great deal of apprehension with regard to the outcome of the congressional election. To ensure the continuance of the legal-juridical edifice needed to protect the extreme neoliberal economic model, as well as the class alliance that was the dictatorship's greatest accomplishment, the Pinochet regime promulgated a new electoral law. This piece of legislation guaranteed that a minority could control the most important aspects of the legislative process; more specifically, the minority could block any attempt to transform the regime made by a new democratic administration. In effect, the electoral law contained dispositions that ostensibly distorted the electorate's will. A relative majority was not going to be enough in some cases to secure a victory; proportional representation was also to be affected by a requirement that candidates belong to coalition lists. In practice, this meant that twenty-three progovernment candidates were able to enter the Senate and the Chamber of Deputies through the back door: all of them were elected *even though they received fewer votes* than the Concertación (the anti-Pinochet) candidates. To put it bluntly: they were elected even though they came third or fourth in the popular vote!

Just to illustrate the distortion created by the electoral legislation, the following case is pertinent. In the election for two Senate seats in the capital city of Santiago, the Christian Democrat candidate at the top of the democratic opposition list won the largest number of votes among all contestants and therefore got elected. The other prodemocracy candidate—a member of the Socialist Party—in the same list obtained 399,408 votes but lost to the candidate at the top of the pro-Pinochet list, who received only 224,302 votes. The difference of 175,106 popular votes was not enough to secure the Socialist a seat; for that to happen, he needed to double his opponent's vote. The absurdity of the situation reached a new climax when the elected senator, archconservative Jaime Guzmán, was assassinated in 1991. Rather than replacing him through a by-election, the rules stipulated that he be replaced by the other candidate in his list, even though this individual had placed fourth in the contest. But tinkering with the election rules was not enough: to attain a controlling minority in the 1990 legislature, the outgoing regime set in motion the constitutional prerogatives that allowed it to appoint nine individuals to the Senate—a margin large enough to thwart any initiative for true democratic reform.

In the 1989 election the pro-Pinochet sectors, though they lost badly, managed to win at least one-third of the popular vote. This percentage, when added to the appointed members of the Senate, was enough to ensure that, at least during the "transitional" administration of President Aylwin, the counterrevolutionary regime was to be preserved. An analysis of congressional elections since 1957 indicates that military intervention has contributed to reversing a growing trend of leftist support while increasing support for the right (see Table 6.1).

Table 6.1 Basic Electoral Data, 1957–1989

	1957	1965	1969	1973	1988	1989
% population registered	18.0	34.8	—	44.5	61.0	59.0
% registered voters participating	35.9	69.5	81.2	92.1	94.5	—
Voting turnout as % of population	12.3	27.4	20.9	36.3	57.7	55.8
% rightist vote	33.0	12.9	20.9	23.6	43.0	40.7
% Christian Democratic Party (PDC) vote	9.4	43.6	31.3	29.1	—	26.1
% Radical Party (PR) vote	22.1	17.7	13.4	5.5	—	3.8
% center (PDC + PR) vote	31.5	61.3	44.7	34.6	51.4	54.7
% leftist vote	10.7	23.3	29.4	38.9	—	5.2

The Role of the Legislature in
the Construction of Liberal Democracy

The Chilean legislature is composed of the Chamber of Deputies and the Senate. Both institutions formally participate in the lawmaking procedures. The Chamber of Deputies has 120 members elected in direct election; the Senate, in turn, has 26 members elected in direct elections plus 9 appointed individuals. All deputies and senators can be reelected indefinitely. After the 1989 election, the composition of both chambers was as shown in Table 6.2.

Table 6.2   Party Composition in the Chilean Congress, 1989–1993

Party	Deputies	Senators
	Left-Center Coalition	
Christian Democratic Party	39	13
Party for Democracy (PPD)	16	4
Radical Party	5	2
Social Democratic Party (PSD)	1	1
Humanist Party (PH)	1	0
Alliance of Center Party (PAC)	1	0
Christian Left (IC)[a]	2	0
Socialist Party (PS)[a]	7	1
Radical Socialist Democratic Party[a]	0	1
Others	9	2
Subtotal	72 (60%)	22 (47%)
	Right-wing Coalition	
National Renewal (RN)	30	5
Independent Democratic Union (UDI)	11	2
Independent Right	7	9
Appointed by the military regime	—	9
Subtotal	48 (40%)	25 (34% elected, 19% appointed)
Total	120	47

Note: a. Not part of Concertación.

With this Congress having already functioned for four years, a number of operational questions need to be raised in order to ascertain the likelihood of it being capable to contribute to the democratization of Chilean society:

1. How committed to participatory democracy can this parliament be, given the fact that many of its members were actively involved with the military dictatorship? Have these members truly transformed themselves so that they now support some form of liberal democracy?

2. What types of measures did the majority of Congress adopt in order to undo the restricted democracy inherited from the dictatorship? Or was this parliament mostly concerned with the consolidation of the institutional order created by the previous regime? Were the restrictive clauses in the Constitution lifted to permit trade union leaders and the less educated to run for office? Were members of the left allowed to reintegrate into the political process?

3. How has Congress dealt with the armed forces? Were military officers held accountable for the systematic violation of human rights? Were the armed forces placed under civilian control?

4. How has the parliament dealt with the judiciary, especially the Supreme Court? Can members of the judiciary be impeached for gross neglect of duties, namely the failure to protect civil and political rights during the dictatorship?

5. Has there been an attempt to democratize the economy by reestablishing workers' fundamental rights? Were measures adopted to bring some form of assistance to those sectors devastated by the extreme neoliberal economic policies of the previous government? Has the parliament considered legislation to reassert the country's control over natural resources now in hand of multinational corporations?

6. Were victims of human rights abuse compensated? Have political prisoners been released and political exiles allowed to return?

In short, these and certainly many other questions need to be answered in order to assess the performance of the current legislature. However, there is an inherent unfairness in asking these questions. In effect, the sum total of the answers is predictably negative. However, it should be recognized that this is largely because, as stated in the preceding discussion, the new legislature was engineered without the attributes required to bring about the democratization of society. Instead, it was created in order to provide a "democratic" facade, to give loyal support and ratify the actions of a strong executive, one that at least in the case of Pinochet had no intention of leaving office. There was no real commitment to create a government of, by, and for the people and characterized by checks and balances and an equilibrium among the various powers of the state.

It was the ideas of Edmund Burke, rather than Montesquieu or Jefferson, that the makers of the Constitution appear to have imposed. Their concept of a free society is not one in which the "people," or the majority of the population, can access power. For them, power from below must be fragmented so that an elite minority can afford to rule over a majority. For them, the "nation" (not to be confused with the "people") is not the majority of the population, but rather the ensemble of the entire population guided by a "natural aristocracy."[17] This minority, whose resources are found outside the state, can then control power in order to retain its privileges within a rigidly divided class society. It goes without saying that this minority is less than predisposed to fight for the expansion of political freedoms that could favor society's popular sectors.

With regard to the democratic proclivities of the transition legislature, some figures are quite interesting. In total, the right-wing opposition took a majority (53 percent) of the Senate seats. This has given the Chilean right wing a "controlling interest," or veto power, to curb or stalemate any attempt at altering the rules of the game as laid down by the 1980 Constitution for the foreseeable future. In the Chamber of Deputies the right won thirty-one, or 23.8 percent, of the seats. In total, former Pinochet officials occupied 52 seats out of a grand total of 167, or 31.1 percent of both houses. Until 1993, there were eleven senators (or 23 percent) who during the dictatorship officiated as mayors, intendents, provincial governors, cabinet ministers, ambassadors, and/or members of the dictatorship's social and economic council. Hard-line Pinochet supporters formed 68.8 percent of the elected right-wing opposition in the Senate. When the nine Pinochet-appointed Senators (19 percent of the seats) were added, twenty out of twenty-five opposition Senators (80 percent) turned out to be long-time supporters of the old regime. These included prominent figures such as the late corporatist ideologue Jaime Guzmán, the architect of Pinochet's "authoritarian republic," as well as Sergio Fernandez and Sergio Jarpa, both ministers of the interior during the Pinochet years.

However, on the positive side, the 1990–1993 legislature deserves credit for at least trying to deal with some of the questions indicated above.[18] The executive-congressional coalition succeeded in promulgating an amnesty law that allowed for the release of most political prisoners.[19] New labor legislation was also passed in order to facilitate the organization of trade unions. Similarly, a new law came to mitigate the dismal state in which the government found the national education system. Legislation was also approved to ease the reintegration of the many Chilean political refugees scattered all over the world. More significant, though, was the enactment of legislation leading to the holding of direct elections at the municipal level in 1992. Highly symbolic yet still quite effective was the Congress's constitutional accusation of a senior justice. In effect, Supreme Court judge Hernan Cereceda was impeached along with two other colleagues and the army's general-auditor. In the end, only Justice Cereceda was removed from the country's highest court, not on the basis of the original charge of notable dereliction of duties on matters of human rights, but on the more prosaic charge of corruption.[20]

On the negative side, a package of constitutional amendments aimed at delinking the nascent democracy from its authoritarian past was soundly defeated by the minority right-wing caucus. The government initiative included attempts at bringing the armed forces under civilian control, reinstating the presidential powers over military appointments, recovering the right to oversee the armed forces' annual budget, and passing a new electoral law. Equally important was the inability of the minority-controlled parliament to pass legislation aimed at bringing to justice those members of the armed forces known to have violated human rights. It was at this time that the fail-safe mechanisms incorporated into the 1980 Constitution came to be seen as an albatross around the new democracy's neck. The inability to undo the authoritarian institutional order became a source of frustration for the president and the democratic coalition. Both Aylwin and the president of the Senate, Gabriel Valdes, openly decried the undemocratic nature of the inherited institutionality.[21] Predictably, their complaints were rejected outright by the Supreme Court and the armed forces. A government campaign to make the Supreme Court accountable for its abandonment of duties during the dictatorship years came to a head when the highest tribunal issued a public statement accusing the government of creating a situation that imperiled the institutional order and the rule of law. Aware that a similar statement in August 1973 had paved the way for the military coup, the Aylwin government backed down in the intensity of its denunciations against the judiciary, although it continued to advocate the "modernization" of this institution.

As for military-civilian relations during this first legislature, the executive-congressional coalition pursued a very simple strategy. It concentrated its efforts in trying to distance General Pinochet from his subordinates in the armed forces. This approach met only with mild success because the majority within the military continued to give their unconditional support to the former dictator. The latter, in turn, did not flinch by any means. He adamantly maintained that his permanence at the helm of the military was necessary in order to protect *his fellow soldiers.* When a report on human rights violations during his years in power was published by the Commission of Reconciliation and Truth, General Pinochet intimidated the government by placing the army on a state of alert.[22] Similar measures were taken on those other occasions when a conflict between the armed forces and the executive-legislative coalition appeared imminent.[23] In the end, the government benefited more from the armed forces' own blunders than from any efforts to force Pinochet out. There is now a generalized perception that the military needs to be made accountable to civilian power.[24]

The 1993 General Election

On December 11, 1993, Senator Eduardo Frei, the son of former president Frei (1964–1970), was elected to the presidency with an absolute majority: 57.99 percent of the vote (or a total of 4,044,112 votes). On the surface, the right fared poorly. It failed to agree on a common candidate, so, as in 1989, it ran two separate candidates. The runner-up was Arturo Alessandri of the rightist Union for Progress coalition, with 24.39 percent of the vote. A distant third was the independent rightist candidate José Piñera, who pulled only 6.18 percent. There were also some candidates on the left, outside the eight-party (and Christian Democrat–dominated) Concertación umbrella. Ecologist Manfred Max-Neef received 5.55 percent of the ballots, and Eugenio Pizarro of the Allende Movement of the Democratic Left (MIDA) and Cristian Reitze of the Humanist/Green Party alliance, obtained 4.69 and 1.17 percent, respectively. If one adds the votes for the Concertación to those of the various factions on the left, there appears to be a large constituency (69.4 percent) favoring reforms to the institutional legacy of the military regime. There was an abstention rate of between 9 and 10 percent of all registered voters.

Following in the footsteps of President Aylwin, President-elect Frei has promised "to work to continue to consolidate democracy in Chile." The president-elect has made a programmatic commitment to continue the Concertación's efforts to reestablish civilian control over the military. This "democratic agenda," with broad appeal to the nearly 70 percent who voted for change, involves five sets of reforms to Pinochet's "authoritarian" Constitution. One is the removal of the appointed senators, designated by the Pinochet regime in 1990 and who will remain in office until 1997. Another is a series of constitutional provisions to allow the president to appoint and/or remove military chiefs in all the branches of the armed forces. A third set relates to the Pinochet-appointed Supreme Court and its ability to operate as the center for preserving the authoritarian institutions of the former military regime. A fourth refers to the various parliamentary quorums required for both constitutional and legal reforms to the "organic" legislation passed before the dictatorship stepped down. Finally, there are electoral reforms to permit a more democratic representation of constituencies, rather than the convoluted system geared to giving the old regime an effective veto power.

A less controversial constitutional reform was approved on December 13, after a long negotiation, between Concertación and right-wing forces. President Aylwin introduced a proposal for reducing the presidential term in office from eight to six years. (Aylwin's preferred formula was four years without immediate reelection—the formula he imposed on himself upon taking office in 1990.) The six-year term was quickly approved by both chambers. If it is ratified in a joint session of Congress on February 15, 1994, it will take effect when Frei is sworn into office in early March.[25] A constitutional ban on presidential reelection to successive terms remains in effect. This constitutional reform is likely the only such change for the time being.[26]

Frei has also vowed to maintain the economic and social policies of his predecessor. The "economic agenda," unlike the aforementioned constitutional reforms, represents a neoliberal package directed to the economic right, much of which has rallied around the powerful business confederations linked to both the right-wing parties and the Christian Democrats. Of the two platforms of the Concertación's political project, the economic agenda is the most likely to be implemented.[27]

On the constitutional and human rights front, Frei, like his predecessor, is likely to face great difficulties. A closer examination of the 1993 electoral results would indicate that, despite receiving an absolute majority of the votes cast, the Concertación did not do so well in the congressional voting as to be able to break the logjam. The proposed constitutional amendments are likely to face an uphill battle because, according to the rules laid down by Pinochet, they require a two-thirds majority in both chambers of Congress. In the December 11 election, all 120 seats in the Chamber of Deputies were contested. In the Senate, only eighteen of the thirty-eight seats were up for election. This does not include the eight[28] remaining military-appointed senators, who raise the number to forty-six. The Concertación won nine of the eighteen seats contested, with the other nine going to opposition parties. The government now controls a total of twenty-one of the forty-six seats in the Senate, representing a *net loss* of one seat. Opposition parties now control seventeen seats, in addition to the eight held by the military-appointed senators. In the lower chamber there is a similar situation. Because of the skewness of the electoral procedures instituted by the exiting military regime in 1989, the Concertación won a total of seventy seats. Opposition parties won forty-six, with four seats going to independent candidates. In total, the Concertación *lost two seats,* when compared with the 1989 elections. A comparison of the number of members of Congress in the 1989 and 1994 elections (Table 6.3) shows the relative variation in the correlation of forces.[29]

Table 6.3   **Party Representation in the Chilean Congress, 1989 and 1993**

Party	Deputies			Senators		
	1989	1993	Change	1989	1993	Change
Left-Center coalition						
Christian Democratic Party	39	37	−2	13	13	0
Party for Democracy	16	15	−1	4	3	−1
Radical Party	5	2	−3	2	1	−1
Social Democratic Party	1	0	−1	1	0	−1
Humanist Party	1	0	−1	—	—	—
Radical Socialist Democratic Party	—	—	—	1	0	−1
Independent candidates (left)	3	0	−3	—	—	—
Right-wing coalition						
National Renewal	30	30	0	5	11	+6
Independent Democratic Union	11	17	+6	2	3	+1
Center-Center Union (UCC)	0	2	+2	0	1	+1
Independent candidates (right)	7	2	−5	9	2	−7

Conclusion

Reality often works in unpredictable ways. The limits imposed upon the Chilean Congress have been already circumvented by means of a closer rapport with the executive; this rapport is (and will be for at least another six years) ideologically associated with the majority of those who have come to sit in the legislature. There has been a small resurgence of a popular movement. In the midst of economic prosperity, some minor gains against further destitution have been achieved. Even incrementalism is capable of generating a critical mass beyond which maintenance of the status quo becomes tenuous. The situation created by the 1989 elections would then make it possible, at least on purely theoretical grounds, to accomplish precisely the opposite of what was anticipated by the makers of the fraudulent 1980 Constitution: the ideological affinity between the executive and the parliament could more than suffice to overhaul the undemocratic institutional order that is the dictatorship's legacy.

The lingering question is whether or not there is such a commitment inside Congress. This is especially important given the aforementioned "fail-safe" mechanisms acting as deterrents against "democratic excesses." Another issue is how the executive and the legislature, acting in unison, can introduce the reforms needed to create a more democratic polity. (The elected representatives in Congress could just sit back and complain that little can be done in the absence of a majority or democratic rules.) Furthermore, if supporters of democracy could draw to their side some of the former supporters of the dictatorship now in Congress, the question remains how far they are willing to go in reforming Chile's low-intensity type of democracy.[30] The substantive issue is whether or not those in the "pact of elites" wish to break ranks with their class allegiances and their cozy relationship with an oligarchy that is intrinsically afraid of broader popular participation, reform, and democracy itself.

Notes

1. Speech by General Augusto Pinochet on September 11, 1976, on the occasion of promulgating Institutional Acts 2, 3, and 4. [See *El Mercurio,* international edition, week of September 11, 1976.] It is worth mentioning that the notion of national security permeates the entire 1980 Constitution: it is mentioned nine times in Chapter III (Constitutional Rights and Obligations), eight times in Chapter IV (Government), five times in Chapter V (National Congress), twice in Chapter X (Armed Forces), six times in Chapter XI (National Security Council), once in Chapter XII (Central Bank), and four times in the Transitory Provisions section. In all, the 1980 Constitution mentions "national security" on thirty-five occasions, as compared with none in the previous 1925 Constitution. [See Nibaldo Galleguillos, "The Making of the Chilean Authoritarian State: A Case Study of a Defensive Coup d'Etat," unpublished Ph.D. diss., Department of Political Science, University of Toronto, 1987, pp. 362 and 376.]

2. Whatever the merits of the Christian Democratic administration (1964–1970) and the Popular Unity government (1970–1973), the two are to be commended for their commitment to the democratization of the Chilean society. This can be seen in the expansion of the franchise, the expansion of the education system, the increasing accessibility to universities and colleges, the integration of the peasantry and urban marginal sectors, and many other progressive initiatives. In taking these actions, they certainly drew strong opposition from the traditional ruling sectors who had favored, and continue to favor even today, a restricted form of political participation.

3. Speech by General Augusto Pinochet, quoted in *Chilegram,* Vol. 5, No. 32 (February 1978), p. 7.

4. Ibid., p.6.

5. Article 53.4 of the 1980 Constitution is very explicit in this regard:

A Deputy or a Senator shall cease in his position if he exercises any influence upon administrative or judicial authorities in favor or on behalf of the employer or the workers in bargaining or labor conflicts, either of the public or private sector, or intervenes in them before any of the parties. The same sanction shall be applied to the congressmen who act or intervene in student activities, regardless of the branch of education, for the purpose of attempting against normal course thereof.

Without prejudice to provisions of Article 8, a Deputy or Senator shall, likewise, cease in functions if he verbally or in writing incites to the alteration of public order or advocates a change in the institutional juridical order by means other than those established by the Constitution, or if he gravely affects the security and honor of the Nation.

A Deputy or Senator shall also cease in his functions if, while exercising the functions of president of the respective chamber or committee, he permits the voting on a motion or proposal that is declared openly contrary to the Political Constitution of the State by the Constitutional Court. The author or authors of such a motion or proposal shall incur the same sanction.

6. It needs to be remembered that precoup legislatures made possible the passing of progressive legislation permitting the implementation of an agrarian reform (in 1967, under a Christian Democratic administration) and the nationalization of the mostly foreign-owned mining sector (in 1971, under a Popular Unity government). Likewise, the last Congress played an extremely important political role in delegitimizing Allende's government. It paved the way for the September 1973 coup by unconstitutionally passing a resolution in August 1973 declaring that the Marxist administration had violated the rule of law. As is well known, new military leaders will time and again make references to such a resolution in order to justify their intervention.

7. It did not take long for General Pinochet to transform the government junta into a subservient institution. [See Galleguillos, "The Making of the Chilean Authoritarian State," Chapter 5.]

8. The emphasis on a strong executive power must be seen in terms of a political constitution that was tailored to meet General Pinochet's desire to remain in control of power for as long as possible (until 1997, as originally anticipated).

9. These attributes of the two legislative bodies must be understood clearly: without them there would be no justification for a legislature to exist. They are the legislative bodies' raison d'être. They are essential, in the Chilean case at least, to the formal commitment to the balance-of-power doctrine created by the makers of the Constitution.

10. The epitome of the "protected" nature of the new democracy is the creation of the National Security Council. This organization enjoys powers granted to no other agency in the previous institutional order. Its composition is also remarkable: the four commanders-in-chief plus the president of the Supreme Court. Only two of its members are popularly elected: the president of the republic itself and the president of the Senate. Its attributes include the right to represent to the Chilean president, the Congress, or the Constitutional Tribunal its opinion regarding any deed, act, or matter that in

its judgment gravely works against the foundations of the institutional order or that might affect national security. It can demand that all documentation or information related to the external and internal security of the state be produced by any authority or government official. The latter are obliged to furnish such documentation; refusal to do so makes them liable to sanctions established in the Constitution (Article 96, letters b and d).

More ominous are some other attributes, such as the the appointment of four former commanders-in-chief to the Senate (the Supreme Court designates three more) and the appointment of two lawyers to the Constitutional Tribunal (again, the Supreme Court appoints three others). All the above appointees in turn enjoy an eight-year tenure and cannot be removed from their positions.

A constitutional amendment (in August 1989) added the general comptroller to the voting members of the National Security Council. Currently, this official is yet another of Pinochet's holdovers. Moreover, he cannot be removed before he reaches seventy-five years of age.

11. To amend those constitutional clauses that deal with the armed forces, popular elections, the municipal regime, the Central Bank, the Constitutional Tribunal, the electoral courts, the National Security Council, the 1978 amnesty law for military personnel involved in human rights violations, and the reform of the Constitution itself, majorities of four-sevenths, three-fifths, or two-thirds are needed in both Chambers. [See Chapter XIV of the 1980 Political Constitution.]

12. Unlike Article 22 of the 1925 Constitution, which states that the armed forces and the police "are essentially professional, organized by rank, disciplined, obedient, and nondeliberating bodies," Article 90 of the 1980 Constitution alters the military's mission: the armed forces now "exist for the defense of the fatherland" and "are essential for national security and guarantee the institutional order of the republic." This disposition also qualifies the fact that the "essentially obedient and nondeliberating" character of the military applies to them only as "armed corps." In other words, it is only within the armed forces that the traditional vertical and hierarchical subordination to those in command prevails. A similar principle does not apply to military-civilian relations.

13. See Manuel Antonio Garretón, *Los Partidos Politicos en la Transicion Democratica en Chile* (Santiago: 1985), p. 161.

14. For a review of the events surrounding the October 8 plebiscite, see Cesar Caviedes, *Elections in Chile: The Road Toward Redemocratization* (Boulder, Colorado: Lynne Rienner, 1991), pp. 35–46.

15. For a detailed description of the social background of the newly installed Congress, see Jorge Nef and Nibaldo Galleguillos, *Chile: Le Chili*, special issue of *Canadian Journal of Latin American and Caribbean Studies*, Vol. 15, No. 30 (1990), pp. 298–303; and Cesar Caviedes, *Elections in Chile*, pp. 90–94.

16. See Jose Nun, *La Rebelion del Coro: Estudios Sobre la Racionalidad Politica y el Sentido Comun* (Buenos Aires: Ediciones Nueva Vision, 1989), p. 11.

17. For a detailed discussion on the idea of fragmentation of power within a Latin American context, see Torcuato di Tella, *Sociologia de los Procesos Politicos* (Buenos Aires: EUDEBA, 1986), pp. 176–185.

18. The balance of the legislative activities during this tenure shows that Congress was quite busy approving new legislation. It received some 1,130 initiatives, of which 300 became laws. As of January 1994 there were still 826 bills

under discussion in the legislature. Predictably, a large number of bills were not of the kind needed to reform the institutional order. [See *El Mercurio,* international edition, week of January 6–12, 1994, p. 3.]

19. As of January 1994, only nine political prisoners were awaiting a presidential pardon, a matter that exiting President Aylwin has promised to resolve before the transfer of power to the new president, Eduardo Frei.

20. In 1974, one of this chapter's authors, Nibaldo Galleguillos, then a human rights lawyer defending political prisoners in Chile, met with Judge Cereceda, who was secretly handing down sentences against leftist prisoners from an office in the Ministry of Defense. At the time, Cereceda was advising the air force's military judge. The significance of this situation had to do with the fact that the Supreme Court had at the time declared itself incompetent to oversee military courts and had consistently refused appeals against the sentences passed by courts-martial. Reflecting a harsher approach, Judge Cereceda had *increased* the sentence that a lower military court had originally imposed upon one of Galleguillos's clients.

21. Gabriel Valdes, in a speech commemorating the 180th anniversary of the National Congress, claimed that the legislative body lacks the prerogatives that belong to such an institution in any modern democracy. He added that the Chilean legislature did not even have the attributes that it used to enjoy in the past. President Aylwin, on the same occasion, agreed with Valdes that "our democratic system, within the context of the 1980 constitution, does not show an adequate equilibrium between the various public powers." [See *El Mercurio,* international edition, week of July 4–10, 1991, p. 8.]

22. The recommendations of the report fell into oblivion, especially when a crisis situation developed as a result of the assassination of Senator Jaime Guzmán, Pinochet's trusted constitutional advisor. His timely death occurred precisely after the report become public. All attention was then diverted to Guzmán's death, which was in turn used to justify the war that the former dictatorship had undertaken against so-called terrorists.

23. For example, an incident involving the army's intelligence services had them caught phone-tapping the private conversations of a potential right-wing presidential candidate in 1992. The demand for greater government control over the armed forces was again met by the army placing the troops on a state of alert. Eventually, the Supreme Court acquitted all army officers involved in the incident by claiming that no crime had been committed under current legislation. At the time of the incident, however, even sectors of the minority right-wing caucus began to talk openly of the need to reestablish civilian control over the military.

24. Both the government and Chilean citizens were quite embarrassed when it was discovered that the Chilean army was secretly selling weapons to Croatia. Again, the government was defenseless because it could not punish anyone. However, the incident contributed to reinforcing the negative view of the armed forces unfolding within public opinion.

25. An unexpected situation has recently arisen. In accordance with the Constitution, all former presidents having served their full eight-year terms in office automatically become members of the Senate. Exiting president Aylwin, however, might be ineligible because his term in office was *only four years.*

26. By late 1994 President Frei had been unable to muster the support needed to amend the 1980 Constitution left by General Pinochet.

27. Both the outgoing and the incoming civilian administrations have

vowed to continue the economic strategies carried out by the Pinochet government, in spite of the fact that the macroeconomic indicators cannot hide the fact that poverty has increased greatly in the last two decades. According to a 1993 World Bank report, Chile has the second worst income distribution in Latin America (Brazil having the worst). Almost 40 percent of the population in Chile is said to be living below the poverty line. Reflecting on the minimal improvements in living standards experienced by many Chileans during his administration, President Aylwin has seen fit to raise a critical voice against the extreme economic neoliberalism pursued in the last decades: "The market," he says, "promotes consumerism, creativity, and creation of wealth, but it is not just in the distribution of such wealth. The market has neither ethical nor social considerations. The market often is tremendously cruel and favors only the most powerful sectors, those who can compete under better conditions; it increases the misery of the poorest sectors and aggravates social inequalities." [See *El Mercurio*, international edition, week of January 13–19, 1994, pp. 3 and 4.]

28. With the death in office of one of the Pinochet-designated senators in 1992, the number of "institutional" members in the Senate declined by one. President Aylwin, to prevent legitimizing a mechanism condemned by the Concertación, decided not to use his constitutional prerogative and appoint a replacement. Thus, the number of senators, both elected and appointed, went down to forty-six.

29. Sources: InterPress Service, December 11, 1993; Associated Press, December 12, 1993; Notimex, December 11–13, 1993; Spanish News Service EFE, December 9, 1993, December 11–15, 1993; Agence France-Presse, December 10, 1993, December 12, 1993, December 14, 1993, December 15, 1993; *El Mercurio* (Chile), *La Nacion* (Chile), December 13, 1993, December 16, 1993; *La Tercera* (Chile) December 11–12, 1993.

30. This cleverly chosen expression—*low-intensity democracy*—is elaborated further in a recently published book edited by Barry Gill, Joel Rocamora, and Richard Wilson, *Low Intensity Democracy: Political Power in the New World Order* (London: Pluto Press, 1993), pp. 3–34.

7

Uruguay:
The Legislature and the
Reconstitution of Democracy

Martin Weinstein

It should not be surprising that Uruguay, with perhaps the strongest tradition of constitutional rule and the most democratic political culture in Latin America, should have one of the most important legislative bodies in the region—even in the context of a clearly presidential system. But Uruguay's legislature can be understood and evaluated only within the context of Uruguay's idiosyncratic and unique electoral and party system.

The economic decline and increased civil strife that led to constitutional breakdown in 1973 has been blamed by many observers on the policy stasis produced by this electoral system. Not surprisingly, the restoration of civilian rule with no change in electoral or party legislation has led to calls for both a reform of the legislature and a questioning of the efficacy of presidentialism. This chapter will argue that although some reform may be in order, presidentialism is not the reason for Uruguay's perennial developmental stasis, and the legislature functions as a significant protector of the rule of law and civil liberties even if it is not the efficient progenitor of change. In other words, the legislature is a faithful reflection of Uruguay's political culture.

The Uruguayan electoral system is based on a series of laws involving the double simultaneous ballot, strict proportional representation, a rigid list system, and legislation involving the use of party titles (*lemas*) but with the conspicuous absence of a statute on political parties. When this legislation is coupled with the fact that all elective offices are contested concurrently once every five years, with no ticket splitting permitted, one can begin to appreciate the complexity and factionalization that ensue.

Uruguay's legislature consists of two houses: a ninety-nine-member Chamber of Deputies and a thirty-one-member Senate (the vice-president heads the Senate and has voice and vote). The two chambers taken together are known as the Asamblea General. Members are elected to both houses by a strict proportional representation with the entire country serving as the electoral unit. Within each party, seats are adjudicated on a proportional basis utilizing the d'Hondt system. As I have previously observed:

> The fact that the list system regards the whole country as one electoral unit has meant in practice that individuals put in the top few places on important party faction voting lists are guaranteed their Senate or Deputy seat, in effect reducing electoral competition. In other words, candidate X does not run against candidate Y head-to-head. As long as candidate X's faction does well, his position on the list guarantees him a legislative seat. Exacerbating this situation is the fact that all elections take place simultaneously once every five years. At that time, one voting list may include a party faction's presidential, vice presidential, and legislative candidates, with another list for the same faction containing the candidates for *intendente* and the local legislature in each department (the *Junta Departmental*).[1]

The double simultaneous vote is the key to understanding the Uruguayan electoral and party system. It was adopted in 1910, some eight years before the use of proportional representation, and is virtually unique to Uruguay. Under this system, the votes of various factions (*sublemas*) of a political party accrue to that party for the purpose of electing the president. This system has meant in practice that the traditional parties (Blanco and Colorado) have usually run several candidates for president—a reflection of internal splits within the party, but also an electoral strategy enabling a party to appeal to the widest possible spectrum of voters.

Typically a presidential election would look as follows:

Colorado Party		*Blanco Party*	
Candidate X	100	Candidate F	125
Candidate Y	120	Candidate G	100
Candidate Z	90	Candidate H	75
	310		300

Under this example, the Colorado Party wins the presidency, having received 310 votes to the Blanco's 300 votes. The presidency goes to candidate Y, who won the most votes in the party with the most votes, even though candidate F of the Blancos received more votes than candidate Y. In fact, this exact type of situation has occurred on more than one occasion. In 1950, Blanco Luis Alberto de Herrera received more votes for president than Luis Battle Berres, but the Colorado candidate won because his party received more votes than Herrera's party.

In 1971, Blanco senator Wilson Ferreira Aldunate received more votes than any other candidate, but Bordaberry became president because the Colorado Party, as a whole, received 13,000 votes more than the Blancos.

With the emergence of the left as a serious and united electoral force in the 1971 elections, the percentage of the vote received by the winning party has been way below 50 percent (see Tables 7.1 and 7.2). Party factionalization—which many observers attribute to the double simultaneous vote, the legislation on political parties (generally referred to as the Ley de Lemas), and strict proportional representation for the parliament—has meant that the president is someone who has never directly received even one-third of the ballots cast. Sanguinetti received 31.2 percent in 1984 and Luis Alberto Lacalle only 22 percent in 1989. Bordaberry received 22.8 percent of the votes in 1971.

Table 7.1 Election Results by Party, 1971–1989 (percentage of votes)

	Blanco Party	Colorado Party	Broad Front	Party for the People's Government (PGP)
1971	40.11	40.96	18.28	—
1984	35.02	41.23	21.26	—
1989	38.87	30.30	21.23	9

Source: Adolfo González, *Elecciones Nacionales de 1989* (Montevideo: CELADU, 1990), p. 114.

Table 7.2 Apportionment of Seats in the General Assembly, 1984 and 1989

	1984			
	Colorado Party	Blanco Party	Broad Front	Civic Union
Senators	13	11	6	—
Deputies	41	35	21	2

	1989			
	Colorado Party	Blanco Party	Broad Front	Nuevo Espacio
Senators	9	12	7	2
Deputies	30	38	21	9

Source: Adapted from González.
Note: Nuevo Espacio was formed when the PGP left the Broad Front and was joined in an electoral coalition by the Christian Democrats and Civic Union.

The relationship of the executive and the legislature can be viewed as quasi-parliamentary only because of a censure mechanism that the legislature possesses but has never exercised. Censure requires a majority vote of the General Assembly and can force the resignation of a minister. Written questions can be submitted to ministers, as well as to the Supreme Court, the Electoral Court, and the Accounts Tribunal. But the preferred procedure for legislative oversight (and to attack executive policy) is interpellation. The dictionary defines *interpellate* as "to question formally, as a minister or other executive officer, in order to obtain a statement or defense of his policy, conduct, etc."[2]

The custom of interpellating a president's minister was established within the first decade of Uruguay's independence. The parliament involved itself in the conduct of the civil war known as the Guerra Grande (1839–1852). In 1880, Duvisioso Terra, minister of justice, culture, and public instruction, was forced to resign under attack from the Chamber of Deputies—the first case of such a resignation. The 1934 Constitution, which was the result of a nonviolent coup by President Gabriel Terra's faction of the Colorado Party and Luis Alberto Herrera's faction of the Blancos, created a Senate whose thirty seats were reserved equally and exclusively for members of the two factions. In a sense this created a type of parliamentarism similar to that of the Fifth French Republic. Ministers could be questioned and subjected to unfavorable votes that in theory could lead to individual or collective resignations. The president, however, could dissolve Parliament and call for new elections within thirty days if a vote of censure did not pass the General Assembly by a two-thirds margin. This never happened, nor would it occur when the Senate was "redemocratized" under the 1942 Constitution.

Ideally, interpellations should be carried out without partisan politics. In practice, they are a partisan mechanism to embarrass the government. An interpellation usually ends with a statement from the chamber in which the questioning took place. The party in power usually indicates that no resignation or change in policy will result from an interpellation even if a negative vote is taken.

A recent example of an interpellation that carried significant political implications involved the questioning of Finance Minister Ignacio de Pousadas by Broad Front deputy Alberto Couriel. The questioning took thirteen hours, the first four of which were taken up by a long discourse by Couriel attacking the economic program. The interpellation ended as usual with no vote of censure, which would have required the votes of fifty of the ninety-nine deputies, though the legislature barely had the thirty-three votes necessary to start the interpellation in the first place. Nevertheless, fifty-one of eighty-three deputies present voted to demand changes in the government economic policy. Whether such changes will be forthcoming has more to do with President Lacalle's crumbling position within his own party and in the polls than with the interpellation, per se.

Parliament has recently exhibited another role that might give the left pause in its desire to move the political system away from presidentialism. The Colorado and Blanco majority, in a most unusual action, nullified key provisions of the property and income tax changes initiated and passed by the departmental government in Montevideo. On paper the issue was a question of whether property and income taxes could be made progressive by the municipality. What was really in play was a test of strength between the popular, socialist mayor of Montevideo, Tabaré Vázquez, and the Blanco and Colorado leadership.

The Broad Front, as the leftist coalition is known, and the splinter democratic socialists under the leadership of Senator Hugo Batalla of the Party for the People's Government (PGP) have championed strengthening of the legislature, but with the failure of the Lacalle government, the Front can legitimately think of replacing the Blancos as the second most powerful party in Uruguay. The question then is whether the left will try to capture the presidency—a difficult task for 1994 given the Colorado candidacy of ex-president Sanguinetti. Or will the left emphasize reform that will strengthen a legislature in which, even with electoral growth, it will surely be a minority?

The historic role of the parliament as a defender of the rule of law is elegantly captured by Luis Eduardo González:

> The importance of the purely institutional factor beyond the effect of personal attributes is underscored by the role parliament played in both coups. In both 1933 and 1973 the breakdown followed clashes between the legislature and the president, and in both cases parliamentary majorities denied what the presidents were asking from them; the legislatures were an obstacle to presidential will, and their last sessions before their illegal dissolutions, which marked the final step of the respective crises, recorded their anti-authoritarian stance. Although inefficiently and too late the legislatures stood for democracy against the presidents who did not.[3]

In the events leading up to the 1973 coup, President Bordaberry managed to get a tough security law through the legislature in 1972. Nevertheless, presidential-congressional and military-congressional relations continued to deteriorate. A truly draconian, omnibus national security bill, the name of which was changed from Emergency Powers Law to the Law for the Consolidation of the Peace, languished in Congress. In March 1973 the armed forces publicly condemned the political class for failing to help the president in his struggles against the Tupamaros and for national reconciliation. Congressional reluctance to lift the immunity for Broad Front senator Enrique Erro, whom the military accused of complicity with the Tupamaros, led to a military communiqué on May 14, 1973, that condemned Congress for its inability to attack corruption and its criticism of the armed forces. The flash point was reached in late June when Congress refused to impeach Senator Erro and the Senate voted to investigate charges of torture against the military. In fact, some three years earlier, a congressional investigation had harshly condemned the use of torture by police and armed forces personnel:

> The application of tortures in different forms is a *normal, frequent, and habitual occurrence.* . . . It is also clear that the High Command lack energy and courage, if it is not at times an accomplice, in transforming the prisons into places where the human being undergoes tortures incompatible with our democracy, our style of life and degree of civilization.[4]

Matters were further complicated for President Bordaberry when a defection of one of the Colorado Party factions left him without a working majority in Congress. This meant that the executive would not have the necessary votes to continue a year-old suspension of civil liberties and could not get passage of its security legislation. Thus, the *autogolpe*—the military-backed presidential coup that took place on June 27, 1973—can be seen as a conflict over the limits of executive and legislative power; this conflict resulted in intolerable tension between Congress and the presidential-military axis that had emerged in the midst of the struggle against the Tupamaros and the growing labor and student unrest resulting from almost two decades of inflation and economic decline.

In 1968, when the militarization of public employees (the "calling up" of workers into the army, with the ensuing threat that they could be tried for desertion if they did not report to work) was extended to the private sector—bank workers—Amílcar Vasconcellos, a liberal Colorado senator, denounced the action as the equivalent of slavery.[5] The parliament's acquiescence, despite bitter debate, in the use of the military to deal with civil unrest and Tupamaro activity would prove to be a big mistake. The use of the military against striking workers starting in 1968, the ceding of control over the campaign against the guerrillas to the armed forces in 1971, and the turning over of part of the judicial system to military courts in 1972 all increased the military's political role and gave them a signal that they could demand more powers.

By February 1973, when President Bordaberry agreed to the military's demand for the creation of an armed forces–dominated National Security Council, he had little support among politicians of all political stripes. The lack of faith in or defense of Bordaberry and Uruguay's political institutions in general was exemplified by a bitter debate in the Senate in the aftermath of the crisis.[6] The coup would come four months later and would rupture constitutional government for more than eleven years.

In the first year of restored constitutional rule, there was an overwhelming desire by the parliament to cooperate with the executive, as exemplified by Blanco leader Wilson Ferreira Aldunate's pledge to provide "governability" to the Sanguinetti administration. The common desire for institutionalization of a restored democracy took primacy over any differences between the legislative and executive power or the political parties.

Faithful to Uruguay's democratic political culture, parliament passed a law sponsored by the president that pardoned the remaining political prisoners, including the leaders of the Tupamaro guerrilla movement. Another law nullified many of the acts passed by the Council of State, which had served as the legislative arm of the military dictatorship. Further legislation created a sorely needed national administration for public education. Toward the end of this first legislative session under restored democracy, the parliament passed a law that permitted the rehiring of public employees who had been summarily dismissed by the military regime. All of this legislation was supported by the executive and justified as an act of "national pacification" or "legal reparation."

By the end of 1985, signs of strain in executive-legislative relations emerged with the interpellation of the minister of interior. The year 1986 was taken up by attempts to deal with the legacy of human rights violations by the military during its nearly twelve years of rule. This fierce debate contributed to the highly unusual failure of the parliament to pass the budget authorization for the following year, the annual legislation known as Rendición de Cuentas. The year 1986 ended with the last-minute approval of a controversial amnesty law (on December 2, 1986) that exonerated all police and armed forces personnel for human rights violations committed between 1973 and 1985. It was this legislation that led to the human rights plebiscite that took place in April 1989.

The last three years of the Sanguinetti government saw deterioration in executive-legislative relations as well as increased caution on the part of the executive. The result was that no important legislation was passed in the period leading up to the November 1989 elections.

The election of Blanco president Luis Alberto Lacalle increased the legislative agenda but further strained executive-legislative relations because of Lacalle's neoliberal, free-market economic agenda, which was coupled with severe fiscal restraints. Several pieces of major legislation sat in Congress for periods of up to one year, and after much debate and delay the president could claim some victories. Some port services were privatized, passenger railroad service (used by very few people) was eliminated, and legislation was passed enabling the government to privatize state enterprises including the airline (PLUNA) and the telephone company (ANTEL).

It was this last piece of legislation that produced a call for a referendum on the law authorizing the sale of ANTEL and other public enterprises. The law's opponents ultimately succeeded in getting the issue before the voters in a plebiscite that took place on December 13, 1992. The overwhelming rejection of privatization—and by implication, of Lacalle's performance as president—by a 72 percent majority brought the administration's program to a halt, split the Blanco Party, and called into question the legitimacy and responsiveness of a parliament that, after all, had approved the law in question. Stasis in Uruguay had reached a new plateau.

Luis Eduardo González argues for the adoption of a parliamentary system in Uruguay. To do so, he, like others who share his views, points to the parliamentary characteristics of the system (and the fact that Uruguay's two coups in this century—the *dictablanda* of 1933 and the *dictadura* of 1973—both occurred under pure presidentialism and not during the two experiments with a multiperson presidency known as the *colegiado*).[7] However, the specific arguments concerning executive-legislative relations could also be made for the most successful presidential system in history, that of the United States. Certainly reform of party and electoral laws would be a positive for decisionmaking and presidential-legislative relations in Uruguay. But the issue is not presidentialism versus parliamentarism, Juan Linz notwithstanding. The issue concerns leadership, vision, and the ability to achieve consensus.

González sees the fractionalization of Uruguay's traditional parties as the principal reason for the lack of a coherent policy that could overcome Uruguay's development crisis. That crisis, coupled with a less than democratic president, becomes the foundation for the breakdown of constitutional rule.

On the one hand, the old, peculiar combination of power resources and pressures Uruguayan quasi-presidentialism deposited on the shoulders of the president had been reinforced by the 1966 constitutional reform; on the other hand, the complexities of party government with a highly fractionalized governing party had been aggravated because the increasing fragmentation of the party system had transformed the incumbent, "major" parties into bare legislative pluralities. Chances of reaching a parliamentary majority within the existing rules became rather remote. When these structural factors were coupled with a scarcely democratic president, politically weak and increasingly isolated within his own party, the 1973 coup finally came.[8]

González's somewhat convoluted discussion of whether Uruguay is a quasi-presidential or quasi-parliamentary system begs for an answer. As González ultimately concludes, Uruguay's system is clearly presidential, with a legislature that can interpellate ministers and can also censure them, though it never has. What we are dealing with is a system that, because of its grounding in a democratic political culture, its adherence to law, and its convoluted electoral legislation, produces a president whose party does not have a majority in the parliament, and a legislature with significant power and influence. Rather than engaging in a discussion to "name that system," we could better spend our time looking at the relationship of the president to his or her party, the separation of institutions sharing powers, the qualities of leadership, and the underlying political culture.

As Uruguay's father of modern sociology, Aldo Solari, comments: "A great many Uruguayans, and almost all of the political and intellectual elites, have believed, throughout our national history, in the magic of legal solutions with the most dogged stubbornness and despite repeated frustrations. I am fearful of the measure of escapism that seems to be involved in the transcendence that nowadays tends to be attributed to a reform of the electoral system."[9]

Should Uruguay's parties be more coherent? Yes. Should the president command a majority in the legislature? That would be nice. Should the party and electoral legislation be changed to help ensure the above? Maybe, but don't bet on it occurring, and even if it did, such changes might prove no more effective in solving Uruguay's problems than the switch to a collegial executive in the 1950s and the return to a single executive in the 1960s.

The use of the plebiscite in recent years calls into question the ability of the parliament to resolve "hot" political and economic issues and even the legitimacy of its decisions when it has acted to do so. The Uruguayan Constitution permits a referendum (or plebiscite) on any law passed by the parliament, provided one-fourth of all those registered to vote demand (through their signature on a petition or by a ballot supervised by the electoral court) a national vote on the law or sections of the law in question.

The 1989 plebiscite on human rights sought to overturn the amnesty law for the military that was passed by Congress in December 1986. This law represented a successful third and last-minute attempt by the Sanguinetti government to get an amnesty passed before a constitutional crisis was provoked by the failure of military personnel to appear in court for human rights trials. After a torturous signature collection and verification process, the plebiscite took place in April 1989. It proved a victory for the law's supporters, with some 58 percent voting to uphold the amnesty, albeit in the face of threats from the military and pleas from the government not to turn the clock back—pleas that, though successful, cost the Colorado Party votes in the November national elections. The plebiscite mechanism was used again concurrently with the 1989 elections to increase the frequency of cost-of-living adjustments for pensions. This legislation is costing the government hundreds of millions of dollars a year but was popular given Uruguay's endemic inflation.

The most recent use of the plebiscite occurred in December 1992, when the electorate, by the above-mentioned 72 percent majority, voted to nullify the key provisions of the Lacalle administration's privatization plan, which had been *approved* by the parliament after over a year's delay. This glaring defeat split the Blanco Party and has turned Lacalle into a lame duck for the last two years of his presidency. With national elections scheduled for November 1994, and with the policy stasis engendered by this plebiscite, there have been renewed calls for, and much discussion of, the need for political party and electoral reform and perhaps constitutional changes in executive-legislative relations.

In a revealing 1988 survey of forty-nine members of the Chamber of Deputies, a team of Uruguayan social scientists found an overwhelming consensus on the constitutional problems that this representative sample of the political elite felt Uruguay was facing. Tables 7.3 and 7.4 reflect the scientists' findings and indicate that it is the left and the out-of-power traditional party (which at the time of the study was the Blancos) who seem amenable to constitutional change.

In the same study a series of questions were asked in regard to the electoral system. The results in Table 7.5 show a significant and not unexpected difference of opinion between the traditional parties and the left. The most telling result emerges when the question of distortion of the voters' will by the double simultaneous vote is brought up. Whereas only 15 percent of Colorado deputies agree with this criticism, one-third of the Blanco deputies and all of the Broad Front representatives agree.

Table 7.3 Importance of Various Constitutional Issues (percentage of respondents who mentioned each issue as one of the two most important)

	Colorado Party	Blanco Party	Broad Front
Executive/legislative relations	33	66	54
Electoral system	18	7	54
Protection of human rights	25	47	48
Regulation and role of armed forces	27	20	12
Direct form of citizen participation	9	7	18
Structure and performance of judicial power	9	14	—
Relationship and role of public enterprises	12	19	—
Regulation of political parties	17	—	7
Executive relationship with autonomous agencies	—	—	7

Source: Adapted from F. Bervejillo, C. Aguiar, and A. Massucielli, "Elites Políticas y Reforma Electoral: La Opinion de los Disputados," in *Reforma Electoral y Voluntad Política,* ed. by Angel Cocci (Montevideo: FESUR/Ediciones de la Banda Oriental, 1988), p. 175.

Table 7.4 Public Perceptions of Constitutional Problems (percentage of respondents who mentioned each item as most important)

	Colorado Party	Blanco Party	Broad Front
Executive/legislative relations	33	53	42
Protection of human rights	25	20	23
Electoral system	—	7	29
Regulations and role of armed forces	—	7	—
Direct form of citizen participation	—	—	6
Structure and performance of judicial power	—	7	—
Regulation and role of public enterprises	25	6	—
Regulation of political parties	17	6	—
Executive relations with national agencies	—	—	—

Source: Adapted from F. Bervejillo, C. Aguiar, and A. Massucielli, "Elites Políticas y Reforma Electoral," p. 174.

Uruguay's democratic political culture is confirmed in this survey and in polling data analyzed by Charles Gillespie, who concludes "not only that Uruguayans have a sophisticated and liberal vision of democracy but also that they are able to distinguish its intrinsic value from its contingent ability to solve the country's deep problems. Yet they also

Table 7.5   Opinions of the Electoral System (percentage of respondents who
agree with each item)

Statement	Colorado Party	Blanco Party	Broad Front
The system based on the double simultaneous vote has many defects, but it ultimately contributes to the existence of strong and lasting political parties.	79	80	12
The system of the double simultaneous vote distorts the will of the voter and stimulates party factionalism.	15	33	100
The election of the president and legislature should be done on separate ballots while also permitting splitting of the ticket.	15	47	76
The double simultaneous vote does not exert an important influence either on "electoral truth" or on the life of the political parties.	31	27	1

Source: Adapted from F. Bervejillo, C. Aguiar, and A. Massucielli, "Elites Políticas y Reforma Electoral," pp. 182–183.

see it as performing far better than military rule with regard to these challenges."[10]

The voters' rejection of the military's constitutional project in 1980, which would have perpetuated military dominance of even a civilian government, is the most concrete example of the value placed on democracy in Uruguay's political culture. Uruguay's political culture is not only democratic, it is egalitarian. Uruguay's late European migration led to a far more open society than in most of Latin America, a far less status-conscious society whose elite, given Uruguay's small size and lack of mineral resources, was less rich and less powerful.

Philip Taylor, Jr., the first U.S.-trained social scientist to study Uruguay thoroughly in the post–World War II period, is an astute observer of the country's political culture. In the concluding chapter of his 1960 study, he eloquently sums up his impressions:

The student who examines Uruguayan politics ultimately develops a feeling of some frustration. It does not derive from inability to obtain information, for this is readily available in a society in which there is much publication, where the average man is comparatively well-educated, and a tone of greater trust and confidence among individuals prevails than in almost any other Latin American country. Nor does it derive from a failure among Uruguayans to express themselves, distinctly and (sometimes) pungently, about almost any question. Rather, it derives from the realization that most Uruguayans know much of their country's problems, generally understand what is needed to correct them, yet feel constrained to talk and plan incessantly, but without actually taking the steps toward the essential changes which will cut to the heart of the difficulties. It seems an anachronism to North American ears to say that this is a society which is both socialist and conservative, yet it is true. For the most part, its past leaders have seemed dedicated to peaceful stasis within a democratic context. This is a logical impossibility.[11]

Taylor was on the mark in 1960 and would not have to modify his observations in 1993. The Uruguayan legislature is important because constitutional democracy is taken seriously in Uruguay. The legislature will continue to have an important role—as a recruitment pool for future leaders, as a locus for national debate, as a protector of civil rights, and as a lawmaker in the political life of this small country. It may even become more important if some of the changes discussed above actually become reality. But this does not necessarily mean that much will change in Uruguay, for as Taylor also insightfully wrote in 1960: "It has been suggested by some writers that political science is the study of the use of power for *definitive* purposes. If this is literally true, then possibly it can be said that Uruguay really has no politics. Power seldom is used for entirely definitive purposes, for there is always an evident withdrawal from the logical consequences of full employment of announced policy."[12]

The 1992 plebiscite that crushed President Lacalle's privatization plans by a 72 percent majority abrogated legislation that had been approved by the parliament after a year-long debate. In other words, even when a president is willing to use power for definitive purposes and gets the legislature to go along, political culture and public opinion in Uruguay can thwart such action. Uruguay certainly is democratic, but that does not mean that it will necessarily confront its domestic reality or its place in the world.

Postscript

On November 27, 1994, in one of the closest elections in Uruguay's history, the Colorado Party, led by ex-president Julio Maria Sanguinetti, regained the presidency with less than one third of the vote. The left (known for this election as the Progressive Encounter [Encuentro progresista]) increased its support from 22 to 30 percent.

The ruling National (Blanco) Party also received about 30 percent of the vote. Thus for the next five years Uruguay's General Assembly will be evenly split between Colorados, Blancos, and the left. Coalitions or a social pact would seem the only way that a Sanguinetti administration will be able to move a legislative agenda that is sure to include reform of social security, changing the electoral system, and further integration with MERCOSUR, the free trade area made up of Argentina, Brazil, Paraguay, and Uruguay.

Notes

1. Martin Weinstein, "Consolidating Democracy in Uruguay: The Sea Change of the 1989 Elections," Working Paper No. 4 (New York: Bildner Center for Western Hemisphere Studies, The Graduate School and University Center of the City University of New York, 1990), p. 7.

2. *Webster's New Collegiate Dictionary* (Cambridge, Massachusetts: H. O. Houghton and Co., 1959), p. 440.

3. Luis Eduardo González, *Political Structures and Democracy in Uruguay* (Notre Dame, Indiana: University of Notre Dame Press, 1991), p. 48.

4. See *Marcha,* June 5, 1970, pp. 12–15. Translation by Raymond Rosenthal in *State Siege* (New York: Ballantine Books, 1973), p. 195.

5. Uruguay, Asamblea General, *Diario de Sesiones,* Vol. 51, p. 302.

6. Uruguay, Camara de Senadores, *Diario de Sesiones,* May 15–16, 1973.

7. González, *Political Structures and Democracy in Uruguay,* p. 23.

8. Ibid., p. 54.

9. Aldo E. Solari, *Uruguay, Partidos Políticos y Sistema Electoral* (Montevideo: El Libro Libre/UCCYT, 1988), p. 141.

10. Charles G. Gillespie, *Negotiating Democracy: Politicians Are Generals in Uruguay* (New York: Cambridge University Press, 1991), p. 238.

11. Philip B. Taylor, Jr., *The Government and the Politics of Uruguay* (New Orleans, Louisiana: University of Tulane Press, 1960), p. 151.

12. Ibid.

Conclusion: The Legislature in a Democratic Latin America

Martin C. Needler

Idealism, Realism, Democracy

When I was in graduate school in the 1950s, to talk about the desirability of democracy in Third World countries was to be patronized as naive. The alternative approaches to U.S. foreign policy were thought to be either the "idealism" of well-meaning innocents or the "realism" of hard-headed appreciators of how things really worked in the world. The patron saint of this conceptualization was George Kennan, but the tradition it represented stretched back to the realpolitik of Bismarck, a distinctively German, not to say Prussian, tradition that had been naturalized in the United States under the aegis of Hans Kohn, Reinhold Niebuhr, and Hans Morgenthau[1] and reached its reductio ad absurdum in the blundering "statesmanship" of Henry Kissinger.

Woodrow Wilson was the ultimate object of scorn of the realists. He talked about "soft-headed" concepts like constitutional government, democracy, and human rights, the achieving of which he even treated as legitimate goals of U.S. foreign policy. Of course—the realists said—his League of Nations was a lost cause; of course the disputes of the first half of the twentieth century could not be resolved by the methods of the well-meaning, but only by Bismarckian blood and iron. The Kennedy administration of the early 1960s tried to be both realist and idealist, in an ambivalent and sometimes self-contradictory way.

Some of us unhappy with the reigning paradigm tried a different approach, adopting neither the idealist position that national interests should not be pursued at all if they had to be pursued at the expense of human rights and popular welfare, nor the realists' view that insisted on the rights of one's own state to the disregard of the suffering of

actual individuals—of any nationality. Sharing the values of the ideal-
ists, I started from the premise that the only policies likely to be adopted in practice had to be acceptable to the dominant economic interests and make sense in terms of national interests. Reinterpreting
some elements in the U.S. foreign policy tradition, and indeed drawing on political ideas as old as those of Thucydides,[2] I argued that it
was in the narrowest political and economic interest of the United
States, intelligently construed, to promote the construction of democracies rather than to back the military dictators who promised stability and would do the bidding of the U.S. government because they were
on the CIA payroll. I have been embarrassed and chagrined in the last
few years to read statements coming out of the U.S. State Department
of the Bush and final Reagan years that read as though they were pla-
giarized from stuff I wrote in the 1960s. Neoconservative intellectuals,
former liberal Democrats who moved to the right and ended up in the
Reagan administration—the best of them was probably Bernard
Aronson, who became assistant secretary for inter-American affairs
under Bush—seem to have found that strain of democratic realism a
platform on which they could reconcile their old and new allegiances.[3]

Embarrassing though it may be to find oneself in such company,
support by the U.S. government for democratic institutions is to be
welcomed, no matter what the reason. Despite the fact that U.S.
demands can usually be satisfied by a mere facade of democracy—
which perhaps is as much as can be expected in these days when international economic realities place the narrowest of limits on any government's freedom of action—any support from the United States for
the principle of democracy changes the climate of opinion and produces marginal shifts in balances of power that can make a real difference on the ground.

At all events, we are in the most democratic of eras in Latin
American history. Of course, most Latin Americans prefer to live in
democracies rather than to be tortured, assassinated, and forbidden to
speak their minds (although they also prefer good economic times to
bad, which may complicate the issue if the last dictator happened to
be lucky economically); so it is not surprising that Latin America
should have become democratic once the United States got out of the
way of democracy becoming a reality. A recently fashionable pseudo-
explanation for undemocratic practice in Latin America that based
itself on imputed undemocratic Hispanic attitudes and values—without actually consulting any attitude surveys, which all show that in fact
democratic values are strong in Latin American populations[4]—is hardly more than the latest incarnation of patronizing Anglo-Saxon attitudes toward Hispanics, indeed to Catholics in general, that go back to
the Reformation.[5] Unfortunately, in this book, Camp and Wynia seem

to flirt with this kind of "cultural" interpretation in their use of political culture as an explanatory variable.

The Tactical Value of U.S. Support for Democracy

The commitment to democracy embodied in current U.S. State Department doctrine with respect to Latin America displays some traditional but also some novel features, reflecting its adaptation to the tactical needs of the recent past. Consider, for example, the following:

1. A stress on elections as solutions to conflict. Representing undeniable fidelity to democratic principles, elections are more likely than not to result in the victory of candidates favored by the United States, in that the economic environment is subject to U.S. government manipulation. A transitory prosperity can be created where the United States favors the incumbent, or total disaster where the United States wants the opposition to win. Financial and technical aid in the electoral campaign can also increase the prospects of victory for the favored side.

2. The separation of armies from police forces. This was a clever gimmick that provided a solution for the impasse over the rebel FMLN's demands that its forces be incorporated into the Salvadoran army and that the various repressive internal security forces be disbanded. The peace agreement—not yet honored in toto—provided for a new civilian police force that would include ex-FMLN combatants. A similar solution is in prospect for Nicaragua, where the Sandinistas would retain predominance in a nonpartisan army, whose role would be restricted vis-à-vis a new civilian police force.

3. A stress on human rights. One of the great conceptual successes of the Carter administration, this emphasis made it possible to yoke together traditional liberals and progressives with hard-line anticommunists like Carter's national security advisor, Zbigniew Brzezinski. The secret of why it can be accepted into standard U.S. policy is that serious criticism can be directed against regimes that are out of favor, while only pro forma representations for the record are made to favored regimes. This is illustrated by the sorry record of State Department connivance in the cover-up of Salvadoran government human rights violations[6] while great weeping and gnashing of teeth accompanied any Cuban or Nicaraguan deviations from rectitude.

The new emphasis on constitutional democracy seems to move comfortably in harness with the free-market ideology that regained its self-confidence in the Reagan years, so that a certain air of quasi-constitutional propriety surrounds such current demands as that central banks be given independence from political authorities. But although it is easy for a Latin American to scoff at the new acceptance of democracy in U.S. policy as just another facade for continued foreign hegemony and class rule, the current democratic era in Latin America may represent a genuinely new stage in the political evolution of the region. That is suggested, at least, by the fact that two presidents removed from office during the 1990s, Collor de Mello in Brazil and Pérez in Venezuela, were impeached and not overthrown in military coups.

The Functions of the Legislature

In general it can be said that the major functions of a legislative body are as follows:

1. Obviously, its primary purpose is to pass laws. This is not to say that the legislature itself writes the laws. The U.S. Congress is unusual in that legislative acts are actually created out of the interplay that takes place in the legislative body. Typically, the legislature serves rather to ratify and legitimate legislative drafts prepared elsewhere— by the party leadership, by the president and his or her staff, by a cabinet department, or sometimes by an interest group. Normally, in Latin American presidential systems, the president can be expected to have a majority in the congress, and it is his or her legislation that is passed. This is less true in Chile, where there is normally a multiparty balance in the legislature, and least true in Brazil, where parties are not only multiple but poorly disciplined.

2. The legislature serves to legitimize not only individual laws, but also the political system as a whole. The congress is elected by popular vote and thus exemplifies the democratic character of the political system, at least to the extent that elections are believed generally fair and the electoral system acceptably representative, in an era in which democratic ideology is the only one generally acceptable. If everybody feels adequately represented in the parliament, people are less likely to be tempted to revolt in order to be heard; the feeling that the Mexican presidential elections of 1988 were rigged, and that Carlos Salinas was thus not a legitimate president, was a key factor leading to the Zapatistas' rebellion in Mexico at the beginning of 1994. This legitimation function is performed only weakly where legislative representatives are perceived as part of an alien caste of self-perpetuating unrepresentative politicians.

3. In parliamentary systems the legislature serves as a sort of continuing electoral college for the prime minister and cabinet. However,

the congress also functions intermittently as an electoral college in Latin American presidential systems. In Chile, Peru, and Bolivia, for example, it chooses from among the top presidential candidates when none wins an absolute majority of the popular vote. This electoral college function is also served when the congress impeaches and convicts a president, removing him or her legally from office. As noted above, this has happened recently in Brazil and Venezuela. Similarly, the legislature may act to fill a vacancy in the presidency caused by unusual or extralegal developments, as it did in 1993 in Guatemala when President Jorge Díaz Serrano acted unconstitutionally in trying to close the legislative body.

4. The legislature also monitors the executive branch, in the sense of interpellating cabinet ministers and conducting investigations. The congressional investigating committee has caught on especially in Brazil.

5. A function exercised in different degrees in different parliamentary institutions is that of educating the public. Where debates are serious, well informed, and well reported, parliamentary discussions can serve to clarify issues and inform the public, raising the quality of political contestation in the society. In general, the quality of legislative debate has shown some improvement in Latin America in recent years, but improvement has been uneven, and in many countries legislative speeches are primarily statements of position, often emotional and prejudiced, adding not at all to the enlightenment of the public.

6. To some extent service in the legislature can play a significant role in the socialization and training of politicians, who may learn more about the substance of issues and about techniques of negotiation and public relations. It is a place where they are scouted for higher office by party leaders, have the opportunity of building a national public following, and build up specialized expertise by serving on committees.

7. The tie with the voters implicit in the election of legislative representatives gives the voter a channel other than that of the administrative bureaucracy to protect individual interests and get mistakes rectified. Constituency service may appear little more than an errand-running function, with nothing of the dignity of the making of grand national policy, but actions on behalf of the petitions of wronged individuals may prove, for many members of the legislature, to be their most important contribution.

The Relative Power of Legislatures

The relative power of a legislative body is difficult to assess for a variety of reasons—some of them having to do with problems of definition. However, as a first approximation, we can stipulate sets of circumstances that affect the power of the legislature as follows:

1. In the sense of formal constitutional attributions of power, the legislature is stronger where the president is weaker. In Chile, Costa Rica, and Uruguay, constitutional constraints are placed on the power of the president that enhance the relative power of the congress.

2. Where political parties are stronger, legislatures will be weaker in the sense that legislation will be drafted by the party leadership, usually outside the legislature, and party discipline will ensure that the legislation is passed without amendment or modification by the assembly. In practice, this represents too stark a picture, and even where there is a legislative majority of a strong and disciplined party, the views of legislative leaders are taken into account when bills are drafted.

3. In terms of stage of development, the assembly is stronger in the era when power has been wrested away from an all-powerful executive, but before a complete transition to mass democracy gives power to the party outside parliament. In Latin America, Haiti and to some extent Paraguay represent the extreme of executive dominance, although we are talking here about a military-controlled executive and not a hereditary monarch, as would be found in the analogous case in Europe. Nor has any Latin American country remained consistently in the stage of mass democracy in which the legislature only registers the legislative will of the people as expressed in the last election; in some periods and in some countries this has also been the case in Western Europe.

4. A national legislature may develop a strong role in a political system that requires continuous mediation among the interests of sections of the country. The classic case here is the role of the U.S. Senate in the days when Webster, Clay, and Calhoun negotiated the compromises that kept the U.S. union together. Effects of this type have at times been visible in Latin America, particularly in Bolivia, Colombia, and Nicaragua, and sometimes in Ecuador.

5. The case is somewhat different, although it also implies an enhancement of the importance of the legislature, in a federal system where the distribution of the population and the structure of electoral power give control of the presidency to the major states but make it possible for second-level states frozen out of the presidency to dominate the congress. In the United States, for about a hundred years following the Civil War, the presidency was dominated by New York and Ohio, with Ohio beginning to yield, toward the latter part of the peri-

od, to California. Because committee leaderships were determined by seniority, however, the Southern states dominated in the Senate. Massachusetts and Texas-plus-Oklahoma were able to emerge into a dominant role in the House of Representatives, however, through control of the speakership. Brazil exhibited a similar pattern under the Old Republic, when Rio Grande do Sul and the states of the Northeast held power in the legislature, even though Saõ Paulo and Minas Gerais controlled the presidency.

6. The legislature is stronger where the country is not dominated by a single economic interest that exercises an ineluctable influence on the direction of national policy. The strength of the coffee industry in El Salvador, or the sugar industry in prerevolutionary Cuba and (until recently) in the Dominican Republic, means that limits are set to the autonomy of the legislative body.

As can be seen from the foregoing, it is problematic to talk about the relative power of the legislature, in that the power of the legislature is seldom wielded by that body as a whole, but by strong individuals—committee chairs, party leaders, power brokers—on behalf of specific interests. Even though the legislature is supposed to represent the popular will, its power may be used undemocratically, for example, by a committee chair who represents private or sectional interests and uses the power of his or her position to insist on changes in policy by the executive, or who inserts provisions in a bill designed to favor some particular interest.

In this sense, perhaps the legislative body as such is at its strongest in a situation of oligarchic democracy, most clearly represented in Latin America by Colombia or nineteenth-century Chile. A limited electorate made it possible for local notables to have safe seats, which gave them a measure of independence from party discipline. Historical circumstances had determined that the army played a lesser role than elsewhere in Latin America, and they made a jealous defense of parliamentary prerogative against the executive feasible. A pluralism of economic and regional interests gave further latitude for autonomy.

This is the kind of situation idealized by José Ortega y Gasset in his *Revolt of the Masses*. One of course has to recognize that those circumstances assumed an oligarchic control of society, as well as voiceless and exploited masses. A legislature in its classic era of power is an oligarchic rather than a democratic body. The most democratic legislature is one in which party discipline ensures that programs favored by the electorate are enacted into law. The countries of the Southern Cone are probably the most democratic in this sense.

An Overview

A concern with Latin American legislatures has, as David Close says in his introduction to this book, been thought irrelevant and even frivolous so long as legislatures had little significance in dictator-ridden countries. Of course, this was an overgeneralization, and legislatures have always been significant in Chile and Costa Rica, and frequently in Colombia and Brazil. To know that, however, required a level of information frequently not available to foreign observers; it was easier to personalize politics in terms of presidents. We now have enough justification to begin to take legislatures seriously—at least where they take themselves seriously.

A serious legislature is a principal arena of political action. It does the job it was hired to do for a democracy if it is appropriately organized, informed, and motivated; where it acts as a check to the executive without being an immovable obstacle blocking the way to action; when it represents the variety of the population with all of its oppositions and contradictions while yet providing the means for their resolution.

At the same time, the legislature is embedded in a particular structure of power, and its role has to be understood in relation to that system of power. The Mexican legislature has, until recently, been without power not because legislators could not succeed themselves and thus build up expertise—although that was the case—but because the political system was dominated by a single party; there was not thought to be any reason legislators needed to build up expertise. In Nicaragua today, as David Close points out, where the structure of power is still indeterminate, the legislature has established a strong role for itself without making itself a mechanism for the resolution of society's problems and without contributing positively to the functioning of the country's political system. The most important general point to be made is that evaluative criteria are best applied not to the role of the legislature taken in isolation, but to the political system as a whole.

Notes

1. Later, confronted by the reality of Vietnam, Morgenthau tried to back down from his earlier position on the basis of a Niebuhrian view that *raison d'état* had to be limited by personal ethics.

2. See, for example, "United States Recognition Policy and the Peruvian Case," *Inter-American Economic Affairs* Vol. 16 (Spring 1963), pp. 61–73.

3. A very good contemporary statement is Larry Diamond, "The Global Imperative: Building a Democratic World Order," *Current History*, January 1994.

4. See Susan Tiano, "Authoritarianism and Political Culture in Argentina and Chile in the Mid-1960's," *Latin American Research Review,* Vol. 21, No. 1 (1986), p. 81; and John Booth and Mitchell Seligson, "The Political Culture of Authoritarianism in Mexico: A Reexamination," *Latin American Research Review,* Vol. 19, No. 1 (1984), p. 118. I deal with this controversy at length in *The Problem of Democracy in Latin America* (Lexington, Massachusetts: D. C. Heath, 1989).

5. I was taught the same prejudices toward the Spanish and French as a schoolboy in England fifty years ago.

6. See Mark Danner, "The Truth of El Mozote," *New Yorker,* December 6, 1993, pp. 106–123.

The Contributors

John Bosley represented Don Valley West in the Canadian House of Commons from 1979–1993. Speaker of the House of Commons from 1984 to 1986, he then chaired a special committee of the Commons on the Central American Peace Process in 1988.

Roderic Camp joined the Tulane University faculty in 1991. He has served as a visiting professor at the Colegio de Mexico, the Foreign Service Institute, and the University of Arizona. He carried out research as a fellow at the Woodrow Wilson Center for International Scholars, Smithsonian Institution, 1983–1984, and has received a Fulbright Fellowship on three occasions. His special interests include Mexican and Latin American politics, comparative elites, political recruitment, church-state relations, and civil-military affairs. The author of numerous articles and books on Mexico, his most recent publications include *Politics in Mexico, The Successor,* and *Generals in the Palacio: The Military in Modern Mexico.*

David Close is professor of political science at the Memorial University of Newfoundland, St. John's, Newfoundland. His major research interests are Central American politics and political economy, with special emphases on Nicaragua and Costa Rica.

Nibaldo Galleguillos is an assistant professor in the Department of Political Science at McMaster University, Hamilton, Ontario. His areas of interest are human rights, processes of democratization, elections, and militarism in Latin America. More specifically, he focuses his attention on case studies of Chile, Cuba, and Mexico.

José Z. Garcia is associate professor of government and director of the Latin American Studies Program at New Mexico State University. His recent research and publication has centered on El Salvador and its transition to democracy.

Martin C. Needler is dean of the School of International Studies at the University of the Pacific. He has held teaching positions at Dartmouth, the University of Michigan, and the University of New Mexico, and research appointments at Harvard, Oxford (St. Antony's College), and the University of Southampton. His best-known books are *Political Development in Latin America, Understanding Foreign Policy,* and *Politics and Society in Mexico;* most recently he has published *The Problem of Democracy in Latin America, Mexican Politics* (2d ed.), and *The Concepts of Comparative Politics.*

Jorge Nef is professor of political studies and international development at the University of Guelph, Guelph, Ontario. He has been visiting professor in Canadian and foreign universities and institutes. He has been president of the Canadian Association of Latin American and Caribbean Studies (CALACS) and is fellow of the Centre for Research on Latin America and the Caribbean (CERLAC) and the Centre for Refugee Studies (CRS), both at York University. In addition, he is currently editor of the *Canadian Journal of Latin American and Caribbean Studies.* His seven books and many articles deal with a wide range of development issues from public administration to terrorism.

Martin Weinstein is professor of political science at William Paterson College of New Jersey and adjunct professor of politics at New York University. The author of *Uruguay: Democracy at the Crossroads,* he has used a comparative focus on Uruguay to write extensively, for the past two decades, on issues of political development, democracy, and human rights. Currently, Dr. Weinstein is engaged in a study of the impact of MERCOSUR on economic development and political sovereignty in Uruguay.

Gary W. Wynia is professor and head of political science at Carleton College, Northfield, Minnesota. The author of numerous books and articles, including *The Politics of Latin American Development,* his principal research interest is Argentine politics.

Daniel Zirker is associate professor of political science and director of the University Honors Program at the University of Idaho. A former U.S. Peace Corps Volunteer in Northeast Brazil (1970–1972), his research and publication focus is on Brazilian politics.

Index

163

About the Book
and the Editor

Legislatures are indispensable parts of constitutional liberal democracies, controlling and criticizing the executive while voicing a wide range of opinions on public issues. This book examines the role of the legislature in the politics of democratic construction and consolidation in Argentina, Brazil, Chile, El Salvador, Mexico, Nicaragua, and Uruguay.

Analyzing the status and daily operations of these legislatures, the authors explore the demands made on government, government reactions to public debate and opposition, and whether important forces remain outside the formal machinery of democratic government—all vital issues in the process of democratization. In the process, they show each nation's progress toward open, competitive, tolerant politics.

David Close is professor of political science at Memorial University of Newfoundland. His many publications include *Nicaragua: Politics, Economics, Society.*